The Capitalist was not very good at talking, unlike the Politician, nor was he in any way attractive, and he did not really believe in anything in particular and so could not inspire respect in those he met. But he did have one import thing: capital, and that means Money.

The Capitalist was often seen licking his fingers or wiping his hands on his pants. He wasn't keen on hygiene, he loathed bathing, and many a person who shook his hand came away disconcerted about what they imagined they felt on his fingers. But few people ever said anything to him about it; he was usually in a position where he had something that they wanted. It would have to be considered the height of diplomacy to suggest that the Capitalist was fat. His stomach was like a fifty-pound bag of cement suspended from breasts as large as an amply endowed woman's, if an elderly one.

All in all, the Capitalist was a thoroughly disgusting man, plagued with bad breath and rotting teeth, and people who didn't know him or had no interest in what he had to offer (in those days, there were still some of those around), if they happened to see him on the street, would quickly hurry by, or if they had children with them, they would shield their innocent eyes and with a sharp intake of breath turn back the way they had come.

BY THE SAME AUTHOR

The Grey Life

Ms. Wellington's Oak Tree

Bringing Down the House

Gyges the Terrible

THE BUNKER SERIES

Thank You For Your Cooperation

Your Call Is Important To Us

Can I Be Of Some Assistance

Today's Edition

The Politics Of Consumption

Adam Wasserman

Second Edition, February 2017
Copyright 2006 by Adam Wasserman
All rights reserved

ISBN 978-1-257-87736-2

www.lulu.com

Part I

The Politics of Consumption

In a large, fortified building on the outskirts of a prestigious, congested city, the three most important personages of Oceania would come together and make their decisions. Yes, that's right, three. It was a rather dull building, or so it would appear from the outside, the color of concrete and the occasional darkened window. As far as anyone could tell it was a single complex, although it was huge, massive, and sprawled chaotically across the cement lot on which it was perched. The entire place was surrounded by menacing electrified fencing and there were gateposts manned by creatures that appeared to be human, although it was difficult to say for sure. They wore thick dark clothing and sunglasses and did not speak unless it was to roughly bark an order. The consumers of Oceania were hardly permitted a glimpse of this building, although occasionally they saw pictures of it in the news, always in the far distance.

Inside the bowels of this building, far underground and protected by the most recent advancements in computer and materials science, there was a large empty chamber. Empty? Well, almost. At its center there was a simple metallic table, round, and three chairs parked unceremoniously about it. The chairs were all plainly similar, very sturdy, and probably of the same material as the table. There was light, too, that came from illuminated panes on the ceiling, and air vents craftily disguised here and there in the walls.

No one was allowed in the room except the three men who used it. Very few people knew it even existed at all. But it did. Deep down in the earth so as to afford the greatest protection from air or biological attack, this was where the Gang of Three would meet – sometimes daily – to hammer out the policies by which Oceania, its government and daily life, would be driven.

It had, of course, always been like this. In countries and nations all across the world, since as long as there have been buildings to house them, there were like rooms with a like table and chairs. The number of the players in the Gang was not always the same, but if they were present their particular characters and natures were more or less similar. There was the

Adam Wasserman

Politician, the Holy Man, and – a more or less recent addition – the Capitalist.

The Politician was the oldest of the three, having his roots in the days when people first decided to dwell in permanent settlements and found it practical to choose leaders to decide on the most important military and organizational matters. But once the building had been built and the room with its table and chairs put in place, he found it convenient to bring in the Holy Man and let him in on the secret.

The Politician was a lopsided man. He had a lean, smallish body and was usually dressed in the most conservative garb of the day. The most curious thing about him was his head, which was large in comparison to the rest of his body. This was a natural and somewhat convenient development for the Politician, his head being the part of his body he devoted the most attention to. The strands of his greasy hair were always neatly and primly tucked into place, and the large surface area of his face provided the ideal setting for the constant smile that perturbed it. The Politician was almost always smiling, and if you ask me he looked absurd doing it, if only because he rarely stopped. But the people seemed very much attached to that smile and would remonstrate him if ever it went away. Over time, the Politician learned to extend it to the lobes of his ears and use various aids and devices to enhance its effect.

Now, as I said before, the Politician found it expedient to invite the Holy Man into his chamber for consultation. For the Holy Man was extremely useful in the Politician's dealings with the people, as they were called in those days, and the Politician had found that the protection of the building's walls provided ample opportunity for stockpiling the various articles of leisure which a person can enjoy, both physical and spiritual. So from a very early time the Holy Man was more than happy to support the position of the Politician, and the two were quite happy with themselves and their little room with the table and chairs.

The Holy Man was more aged than the Politician, grey-haired and silvery (a fact which lent him the semblance of wisdom) and more stocky, too. Sometimes he had a beard and sometimes he was wont to shave, and his body had the usual proportions, but his dress was too ornamental for my taste, and bulky and needlessly expensive at that: long, heavy robes that others often had to help him around in, following after him in a train holding the ends of his gilded garments. He was wont to wear various hats, too, of the most unusual shapes and sizes. The people feared the Politician, but in general they trusted the Holy Man, which is why the Politician courted his friendship.

Now, together for a long time the Politician and the Holy Man arranged the affairs of their various countries and states. At times, for some reason or another, the people grew restless and would clamor, or the Gang of Two (as it was then called) of some other land would assault their interests and the building would be stormed, and the Politician and the Holy Man would be put to the test. Sometimes they were done away with, sometimes one would find himself with a new partner, and sometimes they did not allow the room to be penetrated and were able to repulse the attack. But in the end it was always a Politician and it was always a Holy Man who met in the room in the building, the room with the table and chairs, and it was always they who made the decisions that so much affected the lives of the people.

It is true that at times they were at odds with each other. Such discord arose later in their relationship, and there was even a time when the Holy Man was no mere support for the Politician but actually had him subdued in the folds of his magnificent robe, so to speak, and had the final say on matters. After a time, however, the people found this situation objectionable, for the Holy Man was excitable, and even if the people trusted him he was grumpy and rigid. His imagination was limited to a small set of preconceived notions – immutable and irrefutable, as he liked to say – and his mind resistant to human persuasion. And so with great effort they were finally able to restore the Politician to his dominant place at the table.

Later on came the Capitalist. He was never really invited. In fact, no one is quite sure how he even got there. At first he found his way beyond the fences and the gates and skulked around outside, speaking privately with anyone he met coming out. Eventually, he made his way inside the building. The Capitalist was not very good at talking, unlike the Politician, nor was he in any way attractive, and he did not really believe in anything in particular and so could not inspire respect in those he met. But he did have one import thing: capital, and that means Money. The Capitalist had lots and lots of Money, and because of it he was able to acquire all the luxurious items and articles of enjoyment that the Politician and the Holy Man had already had at their disposal inside the building for years on end. So when the Politician and the Holy Man met the Capitalist in the darkened hallways, they were disappointed to see that their displays of ostentation – which they considered a special treat reserved for only their closest intimates – had no effect on the Capitalist, who snorted with contempt and bit scornfully into a hotdog.

The Capitalist was a man who dressed entirely in black and white. He wore an old-fashioned, black suit with a black bowtie and an off-white, button-down shirt, rumpled and splattered with the remains of his latest meal. His shoes, too, were a shiny, almost unreal looking shade of night, and his pants – which should have been neatly pressed – were creased from abuse and neglect and showed alarming signs of structural weakness. On the top of his wide, balding head there was a black bowler hat, the kind they used to wear long ago when photographs were grainy and still considered a marvel. Invariably, the hat was too small for his head. A few strands of sickly looking, brownish-grey hair protruded from under it, amazed and desperately thankful to see the light of day. These were one of the few signs of humanity to be seen about him. To be sure, there was also the pasty white skin of his bloated face and his pudgy hands which couldn't quite close properly, and his beady eyes, constantly blinking and flicking incessantly from this point to that, in search of more wealth or his next meal. But little else.

The coat that he wore was made of a dark, velvety material and had a long tail that touched his ankles. The tail actually consisted of two parts, two long extensions of material that

The Politics of Consumption

descended from the nape of his back and tapered off by his heels. Yes, he was a man dressed in black and white and yes, silver buttons – and did I forget to mention the thick gold chains that hung from his neck? No, those were not black or white, of course not, and the Capitalist was often to be seen fingering them. In those days he had on at least three or four gold chains, some thicker than others, and at least one large golden ring on the index finger of each hand. He believed the presence of the rings made it more impressive when he pointed at something he wanted.

The Capitalist ate often. In fact, if he wasn't fingering his chains he was either smoking a cigar or holding a bag of French fries drenched in mayonnaise, or fried chicken, or a greasy hamburger, or all three in some wonderful orgy of delight that could only have appealed to this man, such as he was. The Capitalist was often seen licking his fingers or wiping his hands on his pants. He wasn't keen on hygiene, he loathed bathing, and many a person who shook his hand came away disconcerted about what they imagined they felt on his fingers. But few people ever said anything to him about it; he was usually in a position where he had something that they wanted. It would have to be considered the height of diplomacy to suggest that the Capitalist was fat. His stomach was like a fifty-pound bag of cement suspended from breasts as large as an amply endowed woman's, if an elderly one. Several chins protruded from the mass of gold under his face, trying desperately to escape their imprisonment between one of his necks and his jaw. When he walked it was slowly and anyway he appeared more to wobble than stroll along like any other descent human being. He never went up stairs and always took the elevator, even if it was far out of the way and only to go down a single floor. The Capitalist was always sweating, that is true, and his pockets were stuffed with handkerchiefs which, between puffs from his cigar or while he was chewing, he was constantly in search of to wipe the drops of urine-smelling liquid off his brow.

All in all, the Capitalist was a thoroughly disgusting man, plagued with bad breath and rotting teeth, and people who didn't know him or had no interest in what he had to offer (in those days, there were still some of those around), if they happened to see him on the street, would quickly hurry by, or if they had children with them, they would shield their innocent eyes and with a sharp intake of breath turn back the way they had come.

Now, even though there were many right-minded people who did their best to avoid the Capitalist, he nonetheless managed to make his arrival at the building behind the gates and the guards more and more welcome. Once the Politician came close enough to listen to what the Capitalist had to say, he would come more often. You see, the Politician had much wealth stored up in that building, but the Capitalist made it plain and clear right from the start that no matter how much wealth a person had, it was never enough and could always be amply augmented. The Capitalist was willing to help with this eternal problem. And after a time, the Politician was only more than happy to cooperate with what the Capitalist had in mind. For the Capitalist knew what his negotiating position was, although he was always very careful never to state it outright. He needed the Politician to pass laws that were favorable to his enterprises and that would enable him to hoard more and more wealth in his own private accounts, so that he could by more estates, more boys and more women, more rings, more gold chains, more cars, more influence – more of everything, in fact, that Money can buy, which even in those days was pretty much everything. The Capitalist, too, needed the Politician because the Politician controlled the police and the army, and the people, especially when they did not want to cooperate with the Capitalist, often had be coerced by these means.

The Holy Man, on the other hand, was – much to the surprise of the Capitalist – not so quickly won over. In fact, he stubbornly resisted the spreading influence of the Capitalist both inside and outside the building with the gates and the guards. Late at night the Politician and the Holy Man could be heard arguing violently, and one or the other would inevitably storm away in a rage. Other people weren't sure what was going on, but they were vaguely aware of a disconcerting feeling that

The Politics of Consumption

the long standing alliance between the Holy Man and the Politician – the alliance that had guided humanity since it settled in the cities which, the Politician was always keen to remind them, required vigilant defense from foreigners – was under the severest strain. Alone in their room with the table and the chairs, the Politician frankly told the Holy Man that even the gods couldn't stop the steady march of progress, that they could either profit by the change or instead be left behind in those dusty bins called temples, entirely overlooked and forgotten. There are all sorts of elaborations that could be made on the point which I will shortly explore with you, but what it all boiled down to is that even though in the past the Holy Man was known to confuse his own exploitation of the people with the necessities of duty, if someone else were to exploit them he could instantly come up with pretty sounding arguments as to why it was a terrible thing.

Where to begin? Perhaps I ought first to tell you about what it was like before the Capitalist hauled the people into his factories and installed them in cattle stalls and set taskmasters over them. I have neglected to tell you about the people before, telling you instead about their overlords, because I didn't expect that you will believe me, and I imagine you still won't. You will think me overly romantic or simply full of shit, which is understandable considering how far estranged the workers of today are from their nature and the Universe that fostered it. But, yes, the people once existed as such. They were not machines, they were animals, raised by the earth and with senses and reason and instincts that were especially attuned to the various murmurings of the world, so that even if they couldn't explain them they were still invigorated by them. Yes, and the people were once the fertile springboard from which the privileged minority drew its numbers, the same privileged minority whose interests the Politician used to serve, and like him the Holy Man, too.

At any rate – and whether you believe me or not is irrelevant – before the Capitalist lured the people into his stench-ridden lair, the people lived as peasants and tradesmen in the country or in smaller, more manageable towns that were easily escaped. Life in those days was by no means pleasant. They lived in huts and crumbling houses, with cracks in the walls and holes in the roofs and in constant fear of reprisals from bandits and soldiers. Long hours they worked with their bare hands, it is true, but it was useful work, work the fruit of which they could understand and respect. Some were fishermen who went out in boats before dawn and returned at nightfall. Still others molded metal into useful tools like horseshoes and, of course, swords and the like. But most of them were simple peasants and worked the farms, raising vegetables and cattle and poultry and weaving cloth. Some of the animals they raised and they also killed, but not for some small use after which they would throw the vast remainder of the body to collect flies somewhere unseen. No, that would be cruel indeed. In those days the people honored the beasts, some of which could perform useful work, and which even after death could satisfy a variety of wants, so that almost nothing was left to waste.

In those days, the lives of the people were intimately tied to the seasons. In the spring they planted, in the summer they performed other useful work (or marched to war), in the fall they reaped their harvest, and in the winter they slept. They had their festivals, too. Not empty, meaningless repetitions, no, these had actual meaning and relevance to their lives, and they would not have happily done without them. For as I said before the lives of the people were synchronized with the manifold and subtle forces of nature. The people knew when the sun would rise and when it would set, and they could point out how the planets appeared to move in the sky. Everyone had seen a sheep giving birth, a pair of ragged dogs mating, and cocks fighting each other to the death. Even if these behaviors were not their own, the people at the same time felt something comforting and familiar in their proximity. They could name the various kinds of trees that grew around them and identify the birds that lived in them and what sounds they made and what their habits were. Never did it cease to amaze them how beautiful the world was, how delicate (and how cruel), that it fit together so neatly and

The Politics of Consumption

succinctly it was often hard to perceive the individual parts. And their lives being so influenced by the weather and the other forces of nature, it was much easier for them to envision and accept the gods that the Holy Man cajoled them so emphatically to placate. It was so much so, in fact, that aside from the usual harassment they expected from their masters, they were able to subsist on their own. For, when one's work is so mingled with the stuff of life, with the food that they ate and the clothes that they wore and the bricks that made up their dwellings, and united by a certain spirit of brotherhood, the spite and wrath of the master could not prevent them from exercising a certain amount of personal freedom. And although the conditions of this kind of life were often harsh and capricious, despite the fact that famine or pestilence could strike without warning, it was a cycle they could accept because they had themselves been born of it.

Later on, of course, the Capitalist built hulking, fetid factories in sprawling, cavernous places unfriendly to the light of the sun, and all that changed. The people were lured there in part by promises of a better life, duly encouraged by the Politician, but also – it must be admitted – in part because they could not bear any longer the heavy web of often needlessly repressive social rules spun for them over the centuries by the Holy Man. Yes, on the one hand they were choked by them and yearned to divest themselves of their own personal prisons, and yet on the other they associated a certain amount of pride with these very same rules and believed somehow that they had contributed to whatever greatness their particular country had ever had. So the people thought to find some refuge in the anonymity of the city. Instead they found that they had exchanged their drafty huts for unsanitary rooms in huge, poorly constructed complexes with dank air laden with fearful diseases. Granted, they had been cold in their own huts on the farm, but at least the light of the day had shown in through the cracks, and no one profited by the death of their children. Here, in the city, there were no trees and no sunrise or sunset, but there was instead this infernal buzzing. When it buzzed they had to be on the factory floor, and when it buzzed they were allowed a few moments' rest, and when it buzzed again they could stumble home, weary, exhausted, for the few hours permitted. Perhaps most disturbing of all, it always buzzed at the same times every day, relentlessly, unchanging. And the factories, too, were always there, squatting like fat temperamental people that can't stand up on their own anymore, and every day they had to report to the same posts where they were forced to perform the same few tasks which involved the same laborious movements. Time dragged on. The monotony wore down their spirit. Imagination died. And whereas in the country each had known his tasks and had been charged with carrying them out as he thought best, the Capitalist had clear ideas about exactly how one should conduct himself in the factory and did not allow anyone's individual personality to interfere with these notions. No, tens and tens of shallow souls walked up and down the aisles just to supervise the people, shouting at them, humiliating them, and making sure that every scrap of work was squeezed out of them without actually killing them. For as every manager knew, a dead worker could not meet quotas. These men were called "managers" and performed very little useful work themselves, although they were convinced of their own importance.

As fickle as nature had seemed back in the country, it had been exchanged for a far more insidious and pervasive force now that they were on the factory floor. This thing was innocently referred to as the "business cycle" by those whom it favored. And although the people did not at first understand what it was, they could very well perceive that it was harsher and far more arbitrary and served no useful part of a greater whole. But even if they weren't able to understand what it was, they were very well able to observe that this business cycle was a human-made phenomenon, one that benefited the Capitalist and his cronies. When the wheat crop had suddenly failed or their fields covered in locusts, or when an unexpected storm smashed their fishing boats in the harbor, they might have been angry, but they also accepted these events as part of the natural order of things. But not this business cycle.

The Politics of Consumption

The business cycle was the exclusive result of the fact that the Capitalist lent his Money to those who were not satisfied to be merely persons, but who wanted to be important persons. Such entrepreneurs, as they were called, would use the Money to set up their own enterprises, which would usually require the employment of people to perform the actual work while the entrepreneurs were at dinner parties. Now the people simply wanted to live and enjoy their lives, as they had always tried to do, even if they had little such desire to be important. Work is a single element of a person's existence, one of several, perhaps even an important one. It gives a human a sense of worth and responsibility. But it was fairly obvious that these entrepreneurs were not interested in any of that. All they were interested in was paying the Capitalist back as quickly as possible and puffing themselves up like peacocks. As far as the people could tell, seeming important usually meant laughing when one didn't really think something was funny, or otherwise demeaning oneself in order to obtain something that other people would be jealous of. Now, unfortunately for everyone involved, the Capitalist's mood was as fickle as the north wind. There were times when he would throw his Money in the air for whomever could catch it, and then all of a sudden he would decide that he had gone too far, and all at once he would call in his loans. When the Capitalist did such a thing, the entrepreneurs found themselves in a terrible situation (they called it a "crisis") and were often forced to mangle their enterprises or even close them down outright. For the people that meant no work, and because they were no longer in the country, it also meant no food.

The Holy Man saw this, too, and he was distressed. He was distressed because the Capitalist was willing and capable of selling anything, and no moral scruple was sufficient to prevent him from making use of every last avenue of exploitation, however small and insignificant the profit in comparison to the human loss. The Holy Man could also see that the more the Capitalist succeeded in reaping profits, the greater was his influence with the Politician. The Holy Man was a man of ideas and elegant justifications. The Capitalist, however, now had an answer for every argument and remonstration no matter how carefully prepared and would toss it in the face of the Holy Man. Then, he would draw the Politician aside where he would further poison their relationship in private. And, of course, this answer was Money.

The meetings of the Gang of Two became increasingly strained. They hardly sat, the Holy Man standing slouched in the corner, carefully watching the movements of the Politician as he paced awkwardly and intensely around the table, plotting his next move, grinning madly. Every once in a while his face would twitch, usually when he was referring to his own share of the cut. Outside the people groaned and grew more resentful, and inside the Politician met more and more frequently with the Capitalist. The Holy Man was always excluded.

"We have been working together for a long time." The Holy Man had spoken up suddenly, and a bit sentimentally it must be admitted.

The Politician was startled out of his reverie, but he did not cease his pacing. "What? A long time?" He snorted. "Too long."

The Holy Man felt like an aging lover being cast aside. He sighed and stared at the floor, trying in his mind to pinpoint when it was the Capitalist first succeeded in turning the Politician against him. "It's not right and you know it."

The Politician grew annoyed. "You're interrupting my calculations," he spat bitterly, scarcely pausing in his fevered pacing. But he was still smiling. "Times change. Anyway, nothing is ever about right and wrong. You of all people should know that!"

In those days, the chamber was not exactly empty. There were uninspired but colorful paintings on the walls and a few fake plants in the corners with stiff, overly green leaves that never drooped. On the table itself were scattered leaflets and writing quills, and every once in a while one of them brought in a typewriter. There was even a carpet in the room, a rust colored carpet with a simple crisscross pattern, produced no doubt in one of the Capitalist's many factories.

The Politics of Consumption

"We've quarreled before, neither of us can deny that." The voice of the Holy Man was strangely calm, even musical. "We've certainly had harsh words for each other." He laughed then, probably at some small and distant memory. "But this is different." The tone in his voice toughened. "The people are losing sight of God."

The Politician stopped. Standing at the other end of the table, he looked the Holy Man squarely in the face. It was a hard look, an uncomfortable look. Suddenly, the smile returned. "You're not needed anymore. God is dying, and with it you, too." The Holy Man wanted to object, but the Politician talked over him. "A stepping stone is what you were, nothing more! A rationalization of social dependence. Something to help the people get by when they couldn't have enough of *this* world. 'Do unto others as you would have done unto you.' Bah! We have something better now. The people sense it. The people know it. They know who their master is, and it's not that" – a vague, frustrated gesture somewhere beyond the ceiling – "implacable ghost you've been threatening us with! They don't care anymore if it doesn't rain, you imbecile. They care if they are out of a job."

"Their jobs aren't very fulfilling now, are they?"

"Fulfilling," repeated the Politician distantly, his eyes unfocused. "Fulfilling." He seemed, in fact, to be trying out the word for the first time. And suddenly, the smile was swallowed, the face clenched in a terrible rage, and all the blood rushed to the convulsing muscles. "Let me tell you about fulfilling!" the Politician hissed, stabbing the air with a threatening finger. "Not so very long ago you had me on my knees slobbering on that ridiculous robe of yours, carrying it for you, trailing along behind you like a dog! And not just in the privacy of this room, but you paraded it before the people! Fulfilling, was it? Oh, I remember, I remember it well, and now, finally, you're the one who'll be crawling on the rostra in front of me, and it will be my foot on your back. And I'll be damned if I don't go and pick up an axe. Oh yes, you just wait and see." The Politician's eyes bugged dangerously from their sockets.

Adam Wasserman

The Holy Man, for his part, felt strangely consoled by the freakish performance. Obviously, the Politician was ill. Yes, the Holy Man assured himself, he's caught a disease, something has taken control of him. He wasn't himself.

But the Politician wasn't finished. He had resumed his pacing. He had regained his composure, and the smile had reappeared. "You're being replaced." It was as if he were under a spell, and the words he spoke were those of another. "Soon the Capitalist will be in here with me. He's a much more reasonable fellow. I know what he's about. You, you raise the silliest objections to the most important of matters! I don't know how we've managed to get this far, you and I. Honestly, I don't."

When the Holy Man left the room with the table and the chairs (and the other things that were as yet still present), he was pensive. He strolled slowly but determinedly through the shadowy passageways and the twisting hallways of the building with the gates and the guards, his fingertips pressed tightly together in front of his chest. People fluttered about on either side, taking trouble not to tread on his beautifully embroidered robe. There seemed to be no particular order or sense to their comings and goings, but no matter. All the Holy Man saw were shoes, large, dark shoes appended to large, dark trousers, and he saw shadows. He was thinking.

He was thinking about the people. Not because he loved them, no, although he liked to believe that he did. He was thinking about them because he knew they were already taking steps to defend themselves, as creatures will do when they feel themselves to be under attack. Even without his support, even without his encouragement, the people had realized one very important fact: if trinkets and gadgets weren't being produced, or not being produced faster than they were the year before, the Capitalist was reduced to tears and temper tantrums. So, with that in mind, they were banding together and forming loosely knit organizations called unions. For they knew that individually they could not stand up to the alliance of the Capitalist and the Politician, but with greater numbers they reckoned themselves a force that had to be taken seriously.

The Politics of Consumption

And take them seriously they did. For when the people weren't working and the Capitalist was sulking, the Politician wasn't getting any richer. Anyway, internal discord in a country is a state of affairs much feared by the Politician, because anything could happen, and none of it was good. Suddenly, he had to expend a great deal of effort merely to keep from losing what he had already acquired. So the Politician, in fulfillment of his part of the alliance, struck back at the people and their unions as hard as he could. For he understood that if the unions could be broken, the will of the people would likewise be broken, and they would go back to obeying the Capitalist without question, and the Capitalist himself wouldn't be hanging around the building with the gates and the guards so often, horrifying everyone with his disgusting habits and boring them with his woes.

It was this exchange that the Holy Man was now pondering. For although at first he believed the people could not stand up to the Politician's attacks, he saw that their determination made them formidable. He wondered how much better they would fare if he helped them. Naturally he could not openly come to their aid; his position was weak enough as it was. But there were other ways of making himself useful to their cause.

A dark shadow blocked his path. It did not move. Instinctually, the Holy Man halted and looked up. There was the Capitalist, standing in the middle of the corridor, gnawing on a huge turkey bone. And hadn't he got fatter? If it were possible, it would seem that he had. Trails of grease flowed from the corners of his mouth and disappeared among his many chins and gold chains. His girth bridged the breadth of the corridor almost completely, barely leaving enough room on for those who hoped to squeeze by. The Capitalist seemed unaware that he was an obstruction, and the Holy Man, in a moment of rare intuition, realized he didn't care.

The Capitalist was sneering. He was not a happy man. "How's God today?" he bellowed far too loudly for the confines of the dim, carpeted hallway. The large belly encased in the rumpled, black tuxedo heaved.

The Holy Man shuddered. The Capitalist licked his fingers and somehow twisted his face into a most remarkable and certainly uncomfortable expression of loathing and contempt.

The Holy Man – with a mind for his expensive clothing and fancy hat – decided it was best to turn around and find another route. Without a word, he turned his back on the Capitalist and began to retrace his steps. He found, though, that he was unable to focus his thoughts, nor could he keep the image of the Capitalist whom he knew was standing behind, leering, the cruel, cold face of a viper, out of his head.

"Hey!" shouted the Capitalist. "I've a message for you!"

The Holy Man, despite himself, halted once again. Why didn't he just ignore the wheezing serpent and continue on? But he turned his head to the side. He waited.

The Capitalist sucked for a long moment on his turkey bone before he finally belched. "Tell God if he doesn't come clean on his obligations, I'm going to have to foreclose on heaven." And at that, the Capitalist exploded with laughter, vile and somehow breathless, as if it were too much for his crippled body. Out of the corner of his eye, the Holy Man saw him lean against the wall. Between the gurgling and the grunting the Capitalist could be heard repeating the words, as if to those unfortunates who had gathered on the far side of him, not daring to try and pass. He seemed to be quite pleased with his witticism, and later on he probably repeated it to the Politician. Who, we can be sure, chuckled along with him out of a keen sense of his own self-interest.

For quite some time the Politician's army of police and soldiers fought the people, who in turn elected leaders for themselves. These weren't the kind of sham elections that kept the Politician in power, no, these were the real thing, and the persons who were elected after serving for a time in their capacity were content to retire into the background and let someone else with a fresher mind continue in his place. The battle raged for years, for the people proved willing to suffer grievous injuries for the little gain that they envisioned for themselves. The Holy Man offered what clandestine support he

The Politics of Consumption

could, mostly in the form of encouragement, information and occasionally even a place of hiding in times of dire need. And every so often the Politician would catch the Holy Man in the act, as it were, and they were argue, but there really wasn't much the Politician could do as long as the Holy Man never openly declared himself for the people.

But even so, it seemed that slowly but surely the Politician and the Capitalist would gain the upper hand, and the exhaustion and desperation of the people were growing unbearable. It was then, at the last minute, just before it seemed that the people would be doomed to permanent exploitation, that a strange thing happened in a land far away. No one could have predicted the event, nor that its consequences would have such reach and such magnitude. In the end, the Politician and the Capitalist were forced to back down because of it. This is what happened.

Back in those days, the world was divided into far more regions and nations than it is today. Our familiar Gang or Two, for example, with the Capitalist trying to pull them into orbit, was not the Gang of Two of Oceania, because Oceania didn't exist yet. They were the Gang of Two of the leading nation in the region, the nation that eventually adopted National Capitalism and conquered the surrounding countries. They called the result a free trade zone, but it was really an empire. This was the foundation of Oceania, and it was a region that was dominated by our familiar Gang and exclusively served its interests. But I am getting ahead of myself. Far away across the oceans, then, in what was later to become Eurasia, there were also a multitude of nations, each with its own culture and language and way of life.

What? Excuse me? Yes, yes, I know, you don't believe me, what I'm saying sounds ridiculous, but I beg of you, humor me for a while. After all, this is only a story.

As I was saying, one of the countries in that region was a particularly large but landlocked nation that for centuries had lagged behind the other states in Eurasia both technologically and politically. It, too, was led by a Gang of Two, but the biggest difference between that Gang of Two and our familiar Gang of Two is that there was no Capitalist anywhere to be seen near their building with its gates and guards. The Politician and the Holy Man still ruled together in harmony from the seat of their room with its table and chairs.

In fact, they hadn't been outside in quite a long time. They had tired of the world and its problems and miseries and were loathe to leave the confines of the little paradise of comfort and luxury they had created for themselves. Outside the people still worked the land, but they hardly had food for themselves and were constantly abused by the agents of their Politician. The Holy Man rebuked them when they complained and carried away whatever of their possessions had been left by the Politician for his own use. Their lot truly was despicable, especially when they heard the stories of what the Politician and the Holy Man were eating inside the building with the gates and the guards. In the past it had been the lot of the people the world over to suffer this fate, and they had been content, but now there were whispers and rumors of a better life not very far away, and the people of this nation grew jealous.

Well, I'm sure you can guess what happened next. Well, perhaps you can't, at that. An amazing thing, of course, and a dangerous one, too: the people rose up out of anger and stormed the building and murdered everyone they could find in it. They even managed to locate the inner sanctum with the table and the chairs, and in it the trembling Gang of Two. These, too, they murdered without pity. In their place they set a single and lonely character. This was the Communist, of course, and he was a man – more so even than the Holy Man – who acted out of a firm belief in the way things should be without any regard to the way they actually were.

The Communist was a gruff man with a beard who never smiled and who dressed in grey. It was always winter in his country. As a result, he was usually to be seen in a long, thick, grey overcoat lined with furs. The frown on his face was convincing and permanent. For the Communist was a man consumed by anger, and that anger was, of course, the cause of his downfall. Because once a human being acts out of a hatred, even if he is motivated by towering injustice and oppression, the worst that can befall him is that he succeed in his endeavor. For once he obtained power, the Communist showed himself capable of the greatest cruelty. Some say that he refused to allow them to develop naturally, but the truth is worse: he refused to allow them to be individuals altogether.

But he was no barbarian, no. That fact was plain to see in his methods. Arbitrary they were, yes, and unfeeling, but they were also effective. Clearly, the Communist possessed a certain understanding of the human mind and how it could best be manipulated. The Capitalist, for his part, learned a great deal by observing him. But despite his severity, the Communist made an attempt, however feeble, to care for his people, even as he maintained his privileged position in a society that precluded privilege. He educated them and ensured that they had access to medicine, housing and the other necessities of life. For the Communist maintained that even if the people were put on this earth to serve him, there was a social contract that required something in return on his part.

Perhaps you can imagine the reaction of the Politician and the Holy Man in our own, familiar land. When the news was first brought to them, they didn't think much of it. Later on, however, there was a serious downturn in the business cycle, worse than had ever been seen before, and the people grew ashamed of their constant exploitation. They started to insist upon the other half of the social contract, the part the Capitalist was neglecting, that left them starving and begging in the streets. For the Capitalist believed that the people were put on this earth to serve him and that was all there was to it.

Inside the little chamber buried far below the building with the gates and the guards, the Gang of Two sat conferring. The Holy Man in all his refinery sat with his legs on the table and his chair pushed back, and the Politician was trying to support his huge, heavy head and its greasy hair and its weighty smile with two hands and the arms attached to them. He seemed glum, the Holy Man pensive.

Adam Wasserman

"If they came in here, we could lose all our stuff," said the Politician.

"Forget about our stuff," the Holy Man told him. "We can always get it back. The real problem is that the people would be deprived of God. The Communist wants to be the only authority in their lives."

"Actually, we would lose all our stuff for sure." The Politician nibbled petulantly on a huge, flapping lip. "And then they would take us into some basement and shoot us and hang our uniforms in a museum."

"I think we can both agree the evil of Communism must be eradicated."

The Politician snorted and pushed back a wayward lock of hair. "This is all your fault! You promised the people they could have their own lives. Provided they kept buying God's favor." Another snort.

The Holy Man clicked his tongue distastefully and continued. "We've sent messengers, but he won't respond. If you listen to what he says when he's not haranguing the people or throwing a temper tantrum, though, it adds up pretty bad for us."

"Do you think he allows the people any hair-care products in his country?"

The Holy Man smiled knowingly. "Don't get your hopes up. If he comes here, you're not going to get to make a deal with him."

The Politician sat up suddenly and stared angrily at the Holy Man. "Well, then, I hope you have a plan because the people outside are pretty taken up by this social democracy nonsense. What arrogance, to think that they could just sweep us aside and get along better than they had before! If we don't watch out, they'll invite this Communist fellow –"

"Shut up. You're making me nervous. All we have to do is keep our heads."

"Fine. You stay busy keeping your head. I got mine exactly the way I want it so now I'd like to turn my attention to other things, like my survival."

"Our survival."

"Yes, yes, whatever."

"Well, I think we have no other choice."

The Politician's mouth almost slid off his face. "Choice?"

"Who owns the newspapers?"

The Politician was silent.

"Who is the one with the flashy car and the young girlfriend that the people hate to admire?"

The Politician snickered.

"Who do the people believe gives them choices?"

The Politician smiled.

"Exactly. And when we are done with him, we will cast him aside like the sack of garbage that he is and life will go on as it always has."

At that the Politician lifted an eyebrow. "As it always has, eh?" He sounded doubtful.

"Yes, friend. For thousands and thousands of years, and still thousands more on top of that!"

"Whatever you say." The Politician said and sank into vague, troubled thought while the Holy Man played with the tassels that hung from his robe. Suddenly, a gleam of malice alighted in the Politician's eye. Looking up, he addressed the Holy Man warmly, as if imparting much sought-after advice. "You realize what that means, of course?"

But the Holy Man knew quite well what that meant. He scowled and said nothing. It was a situation he would have to endure.

The Politician snickered and nodded his head. Then, he began to whistle.

It was not many days later that the Capitalist made his triumphant entrance. He had to turn sideways to squeeze through the doorway, but in a matter of moments he was within the confines of the inner sanctum with the table and the chairs where no one aside from the Holy Man and the Politician had been allowed since anyone could remember (and that was quite a long time indeed). The Politician had come to greet him at the door, smiling impishly, but the Holy Man remained seated at the far end, his legs stretched out comfortably and resting on the surface of the table. His hands were folded in his lap. He was watching.

The Capitalist was alternately taking bites out of a hotdog smeared with sauerkraut and mustard and wiping his hands on his great, black pants. The Politician trotted next to him during this brief tour of inspection, chattering frivolously, but he was largely ignored. Every once in a while, the Capitalist would smack his great, heaving belly with his free hand and belch his satisfaction. He had no questions. He had no comments. He had no sense of taste, so we couldn't really expect an opinion from him. I imagine he was so enthralled to be standing in that room that he wasn't able to adequately order his thoughts. He did say one thing, however, and that was merely under his breath and to no one in particular, and that was: "We'll have to do something about all this useless junk, won't we?" Eventually, his meandering path led him to the proximity of the Holy Man, stretched out at the far end of the table, and he could proceed no further because there wasn't enough room.

"Why don't you take a seat and we can get started?" the Holy Man suggested blithely.

The Capitalist considered the Holy Man, eyes wide, like a small child being given permission for the first time to ride off alone on his bicycle. No, at a moment like this not even the Holy Man could ruin the sense of triumph, not even he could tarnish the sweetness of the taste of power like nectar running down his face, clinging to his skin, making him stronger.

The Capitalist gurgled. It may have been as close to a good-natured laugh as he was capable. Carefully, he lurched back the way he had come, back towards the opposite end of the table. One tiny step followed another. The movements were sporadic, as if he were afraid of falling. "Well," he sputtered as he moved. A foot scrambled panic-stricken towards the safety of the floor. "I know why you've asked me here. And it's about damned time! I could have helped prevent this whole mess in the first place. But I'm here now. Everything will be alright." The Capitalist was out of breath. He had finally reached the chair at the other end of the table where the Politician usually sat.

Looking down, he saw a tiny, metal stool with arms and legs. There was absolutely no way he was going to be able to squeeze himself into it.

Looking up, he saw the Politician standing by the Holy Man. He was watching the Capitalist with grotesque interest. Certainly, he had never seen a man so fat. He hadn't conversed with the Capitalist in a while, that was true, but even his own imagination hadn't dared to venture as far as reality apparently had. The man, like the Universe, was constantly expanding. "I'll stand," the Capitalist announced, smiling uncomfortably.

The Politician snickered and slithered over to where the Capitalist stood panting, grabbed the chair, and trotted with it back towards the Holy Man.

"Well," managed the Capitalist. "As I was saying, you boys have made the right decision. Just listen to me and we'll be safely through this mess in no time. I mean, who ever heard of it? Setting prices? Government monopolies? Redistribution of wealth? We should take 'em out back and hang them like they did to their royalty. No offense, of course. But it was the only good thing they've done. Now, like I was saying, just leave everything to me –"

The Holy Man tossed an impatient look at the Politician. The Politician's giant head lolled. Two tiny words issued from his mouth like darts. "Shut up."

The Capitalist wasn't sure if he had heard correctly. "Excuse me?"

The Politician cleared his throat. "I said, 'shut up'".

The Capitalist stared in disbelief. No one had ever said those words to him before.

At that, a crude, timid smile crept across the Politician's bloated face. Yes, that face, it was the perfect home for a smile. "Well what did you expect? I'm a master of duplicity. I do and I say what will keep me exactly where I am."

"But you are under attack," the Capitalist protested. "You *need* me."

"No," thundered the Holy Man. He shot forward in his chair and glared across the table. "*You* are under attack." An insistent hand struck the tabletop. The eyes flashed. "This" – the Holy Man's mouth twitched as he searched for the right word – "avatar of the people, this Communist, he may want to get rid of me, but the reality of power will sink in quickly enough! People are spiritual by nature, and that spirituality needs to be guided and channeled to proper use." A quick look in the direction of the Politician. "My old friend, here, too, although perhaps not immediately useful, would find his way back in here eventually. People are, after all, people, and if the Communist meets with any success he will want wealth enough to covet. But you! You perform no useful work. You satisfy no social requirement. No one would miss you if you were gone tomorrow. You are a leech, a cancer, a parasite. You devour everything you can get your hands on and you are bloated out of proportion and you are the most thoroughly disgusting man I have ever laid eyes on. Your stink permeates this room, and I tell you it requires the greatest mental control to withstand the urge to vomit. But you don't care! No one's opinion could possibly faze you. That's why the Communist wants you dead, and frankly I wonder if he isn't right." The Holy Man had stood up and was leaning against the table with balled up fists. His face was crunched in a scowl of disdain, the veins were clearly visible on his forehead.

The Capitalist futilely shook his head. Jittery eyes flickered about, and his breathing was labored. What was left of the hotdog he tried to hide under the table. "I wasn't even over there," he exclaimed. "You were, he was! I never was!"

"Enough of this childishness!" Another slap of the table. "Don't try and tell me whose fault this is!"

The Capitalist began to cry. Huge, renting sobs burst from his mouth. He was staring at the Holy Man with wide, child-like eyes, eyes that couldn't believe he was being spoken to like this, eyes set in a face whose brain couldn't quite accept that his Money wouldn't be enough. And then suddenly his face convulsed and he appeared to cough violently and he collapsed to the floor and now his head was resting between his flabby arms on the tabletop and he was oozing tears and uncomfortable noises and shuddering uncontrollably. The table appeared to be having difficulty holding up under the demands he was imposing on it.

The Holy Man sat back in his chair, a disgusted look on his face, but also one mingled with satisfaction. After this outburst had dragged on long enough he threw a subtle but demanding glance in the direction of the Politician. "You can jump in at any time," he purred icily.

Reluctantly, the Politician began to speak. "Now listen here," he began, his voice deliberate and slow. And who knows, maybe the Politician genuinely felt sorry for the Capitalist, because even if he was a Capitalist, somewhere deep down inside he was also a human being. "It's not so bad as all that. I know the Holy Man talks tough, but you can't take him at face value, either. Sure, he doesn't like you, I know that, you know that, but it doesn't change the fact we're all in this together."

The Capitalist lifted his head and stared at the Politician with red, swollen eyes framed in the silvery remains of his tears. The look on his face showed that he was vulnerable.

The Politician was encouraged. "Now what it comes down to is this. You can hang out in here with us and help bury this Communist person. You can skim off the top like you always have. But there will be limits. That's all. You won't be able to pile up wealth beyond measure, because right now we need the people's support in our fight, and if there is one thing that the people hate about you it's your – well, the fact that it appears that you never have enough, which is especially, well, bad when there are so many who don't have anything."

"I get to keep my factories?" murmured the Capitalist.

"Yes," the Politician assured him. "Most of them, that is," he added after a prodding glance from the Holy Man. "But don't worry, as soon as this situation is straightened out you'll get them back."

The Holy Man spoke up. "We are convinced that we cannot defeat this Communist fellow with the traditional kind of war. There's more behind him than an army. We will have to wage a different kind of war, one we'll need you for. In short, we'll need to out-produce them. It's as simple as that."

The Capitalist was suspicious of their intentions. "And you will still take your cut?"

"Naturally," responded the Politician. "The Holy Man, too."

The Capitalist thought for a moment, but really, it isn't hard for an empty man to choose between nothing and less than what he has. "Agreed." He sniffled and wiped away some of his tears.

"Double," clarified the Holy Man.

The Capitalist's mouth dropped open. He began to stammer. But eventually, he agreed to that condition, too.

When the Capitalist squeezed out of the room with the table and chairs, he was pouting. He felt like he had been treated unfairly. He did not bid anyone a proper goodbye. He did, however, have the presence of mind to order himself a chair on the way out. For even in his miserable state of mind the magnitude of this particular victory did not escape him.

The Politician and the Holy Man watched him slink away and contemplated the future. The Holy Man, although you would never have known it from his cool (if overdressed) exterior, was ecstatic, and was wondering how much he could abuse the man before he should be dumped altogether. The Politician was hoping that the Capitalist wouldn't hold a grudge.

Believe it or not, in the short term things got even worse for the Capitalist. For one thing, the Communist's regime achieved some early successes and did not collapse upon itself as the Gang of Three (as it was now unofficially called) had hoped. It even managed to spread. But, as I said before, the Communist was a cruel and angry man, and everything he achieved or tried to achieve was marred by bitterness and his inestimable suspicion. In the end, he discovered the necessity of moderating himself, but by then his regime had been stained by the habit of repression and severity, and that was that. But all this came later.

And, as I have already mentioned, somewhere among the new wars of global proportions that subsequently broke out, the business cycle betrayed them all. Admittedly, there had been crises before, and the people tossed out of their jobs and homes (it was only to be expected), but the magnitude of this particular crisis had previously been unthinkable, and the people in their despair came very close to doing away with the Capitalist altogether. In the end, it was the Politician who saved him, the Politician who hid him away when the mob came searching with torches in their hands and fire in their eyes, the Politician who gave in to all of their demands except the most important one of all. In that way, the Capitalist remained, and continued to attend meetings in the inner sanctum, even if he wasn't consulted about everything.

I know, I know, it is difficult to imagine anyone with power and stature enough to ignore the presence of the Capitalist or disregard him altogether, but believe it or not human beings were once permitted the use of all their faculties and they did not simply assume that they were made to serve. In fact, people were born then. The rules and responsibilities that governed the peaceful coexistence of human beings all living together on more or less equal terms was called a "society". But, alas, if the things I have already said appear strange to you, no doubt this concept is utterly confusing. Anyway, it is dangerous for me to be telling you these things now, yes I know, and it is dangerous for you to listen. But deep down inside you know it to be true. So perhaps it is best to leave this era and enter into one that will seem more familiar, the telling of which will involve considerably less risk of being grabbed off the street, dragged behind the nearest building, and shot as terrorist.

All hail Oceania, the mother of the National Capitalist state.

There, that ought to buy us some time.

Part II

Adam Wasserman

It was while the threat of the Communist persisted that the Capitalist was able to mould the people into consumers. Alas, this was the single worst and most important development leading up to the present – and the most brilliant stroke on his part, if I might say so. A stunning feat at a time when it seemed certain his ambitions had been irreparably hobbled. For this care-free, self-centered mindset allowed many terrible events to come to pass without so much as a whimper of protest from anyone, and the further they went and the more of the consumers' humanity the Gang of Three was able to deprive them of, the more consequential grew their endeavors.

The consumer was foremost the creature and the creation of the Capitalist, and they adored him even as he reviled them. Not that they minded. The consumer, you see, was notoriously able to craft his own reality inside his own head and project it onto everyone else. In fact, he was encouraged to do this. Invariably, each individual consumer was at the center of his own homespun universe in which he was constantly adored, so it naturally followed that all the idiocy in the world was everyone else's.

Even though the Politician and the Holy Man believed they had outflanked him, the Capitalist walked out of the room with the table and the chairs inside the building with the gates and the guards with his hands firmly grasped around the foundations of his future power. Later on he figured out how to use them. You see, the Politician believed that the best way to subvert the Communist was through military might, the oldest and most primitive weapon of the demagogue. And the key to a successful military is not only advanced technology, but also the capacity to produce its artifacts in remarkable numbers. In the beginning, the production and development of these new technologies was to remain the domain of the Politician, with the Capitalist providing the necessary support and expertise. So, having more time on his hands than he was used to, the Capitalist reached far back into his brain and touched on a creative cluster of neurons. Yes, yes, believe it or not when he

The Politics of Consumption

wasn't in a position to pose a danger to anyone else, the Capitalist was capable of displaying the despondent good quality. At any rate, when he presented these new inventions to the public they fell instantly in love with them and clamored for more.

The Capitalist was stunned. He had never been loved before. Why just now they had embraced him with wild shouts of joy. Why? He wasn't entirely sure, but he was certain their enthusiasm could be used to his advantage. For when the Capitalist looked back in history and saw all the manifold revolutions that had unseated his predecessors when their abuse had grown intolerable, he saw one thing in common: the people had had the will and the means. Take them both away, and they would be harmless. The Capitalist, then, wanted to begin expanding his activities from wartime production to the production of cheap, unnecessary trinkets he billed as clever inventions. Because the fact is there were only so many useful ideas, and far too few for the comfort of the Capitalist's wallet, not to mention that they were tedious to come by.

The Politician, for his part, was enthusiastic about the Capitalist's proposals, especially when he saw the potential in revenue and kickbacks. He especially enjoyed the fact that the Capitalist was arranging everything himself. You see, he wasn't at all sure how the Capitalist could convince anyone to actually spend Money on these products, and he wanted to distance himself in case the venture proved to be a great and embarrassing failure. In fact, all the Capitalist required from him were some new laws and loopholes that no one would notice for what they were until they had long been hallowed and sanctioned by usage. And wouldn't you know it? He happened to have a copy of the proposed legislation with him. The Politician praised the Capitalist for his zeal, and the Capitalist, draped in gold chains, puffing on a huge cigar, winked and nodded his head.

The Politician and the Holy Man, you see, had overlooked a very important detail. They left the Capitalist in charge of his media networks. Under the guise of free expression, the Capitalist was able to use these networks to creep into the minds of his fledgling consumers. The slogans that advertised his products and speckled his propaganda varied in form and word but were universal in their meaning. Draped in superlatives, the language of the Capitalist promised a dreamy nothing, a world with no responsibilities and no need for self-restraint. This mystical illusion was, of course, the opposite of the one propagated in the lands run by the Communist, buried under his great fur hat and all his brewing anger. For the Capitalist was sure to remind the consumer that his every wish and desire could be fulfilled – could did I say? Should is more like it! Let other consumers worry about themselves.

Don't worry about the consequences. Just go for it!

So that's how it started. And really, at first being a consumer didn't feel very different from being a person, except that one's material situation was better, and that was no mean improvement. Yes, for a while – albeit a few generations at most – humanity in that part of the world actually lived in some degree of dignity, and the consumers were introduced to a world where there was ample opportunity to develop themselves as individuals. A human being should perform useful labor, yes, but in those days it was considered just another aspect of a well-rounded existence. For a human being is a sink of all kinds of knowledge and observation, which he acquires in a myriad of ways. The more varied his experience, the more subtle and powerful his thinking becomes. And work is not merely something performed in the name of a corporation, either. Work is any activity that produces something fairly lasting, even if it's only an impression.

We were once a race of explorers and adventurers. There were even some who believed that it was the purpose and duty of every human being to enrich himself as best he could and thereby contribute to the purpose of the whole, that happiness was an obligation to oneself and the Universe and not merely something to be ashamed of. I can't tell you if that is true or not.

The Politics of Consumption

But at any rate, one wasn't expected to pretend to be hopelessly dedicated to one's work. One was merely expected to perform it well. One was expected to show up for his shift and maybe once in a while he was asked to do some overtime, a request which he was well within his rights to refuse. For the consumer was educated, he had vacation, he had leisure time, and he even had some Money left over. It is a wonder that, having achieved all this, the Capitalist through his invention of popular "culture" was able to deprive them of any real interests whatsoever, so that, combined with his propaganda about laziness, the consumer felt uneasy and bored if he wasn't in his workplace slaving away and being told what to do, or wasting it away behind a computer pretending his life was much more interesting than it actually was.

And as for the businesses themselves, they showed much promise as vehicles for growth and exploration, and they opened up doors of possibility to the consumer. But there was a Capitalist squatting at the top of every one of them, a man or woman who behind closed doors slowly but determinedly perverted their aims towards his or her own selfish designs. The consumer at work found himself entrenched in a hierarchy, and he quickly realized that this hierarchy was more important than the work itself. If he wanted to climb up, there was no alternative than to participate on its terms. The hopes and principles he brought with him from university were gradually extorted from him; there was always a higher salary to obtain, a new title with the prospect of yet more underlings. For the consumer knew that ambition never comes to an end, that the most successful consumers were never satisfied with their incomes or the number and impressiveness of their possessions.

Now, looking back through history the Capitalist learned that both the Politician and the Holy Man had devised complex systems of belief upon which they could justify their power and influence. When he saw, too, how useful the practice had proven he decided he must do the same for himself. So, the Capitalist paid a great many people to devise a theory and invent a science that explained why his corporations were a benefit to humankind and not a scourge, why they were in fact the basis of a new and enlightened social order that promoted efficiency, creativity, and justice. He spent quite some time conjuring up his new science, and – just like the Politician and the Holy Man before him – even after he presented it to the consumers (who received it with wild applause) he was forced time and again to amend it. Because economics, like theology, is not a science at all, not even if you try and support it with fancy mathematical equations and squiggles that purport to describe its many rickety and dubious laws.

In a word, the Capitalist proclaimed that the only real driver of innovation was competition. Human beings, he maintained, were inclined towards laziness, and if left comfortably to their own devices no one would ever amount to much of anything. But competition ensures that human beings perform to the best of their ability. Not only that, competition naturally promotes the acceptance of best practices, resulting in the greatest quality for the consumer for the lowest price. Efficiency, he maintained, could only be fostered in an environment where those who deserve it are amply rewarded. The Capitalist frequently alluded to sports and exploits in war. And when industries were still emerging and small, governed by the proper laws he might even have been right. But industries didn't stay small or new for very long, the Capitalist giving himself over to a tendency to merge and combine to form yet larger corporations. As it was, all the players in a particular industry would inevitably collude, erasing competition completely. This was the natural result of human nature, of course. Those in privileged positions eventually come to recognize that they have far more to lose than they could ever hope to gain, or that they have far more to gain by pooling resources than by going at it alone. And although from time to time the Politician was forced to take action against these menacing conglomerates, it was only when some meddling activist forced his hand. Anyway, the changes were always cosmetic and he was rewarded handsomely for it. Once these huge monopolies and cartels had formed, it was impossible for someone with a good idea outside that privileged group to set up a rival. For in order to build anything resembling a competitor the sums he would have to amass could easily amount to the entire personal income of a small country, and anyway the Capitalist was the one who lent all the Money. As for being rewarded, it was an illusion the consumer cherished, and the Capitalist was ever busy finding (or inventing) the occasional example to parade on his propaganda networks.

Because in reality, the system set up by the Gang of Three encouraged mediocrity, not excellence. Products had, after all, to appeal to the widest possible audience, and anyway it was far more effective to spend Money on propaganda than on the quality of the item being pandered. In fact, huge, sprawling departments dedicated to this single pursuit came to envelop the corporations of the Capitalist. The consumers who worked in these departments were constantly obsessed with a thing called "markets". There was, apparently, a market for everything. At first there were only markets for things that were immediately useful, but later on the Capitalist invented "marketing", which is just a fancy and less offensive word for "propaganda", in order to create markets for goods and services that people had to be convinced they needed. But I think I've already mentioned this. At any rate, it goes to show how dangerously ignorant indeed the consumer had grown. Because the open contempt that the Capitalist had for the consumer could not escape the persons who worked these propaganda machines. Behind closed doors they would laugh and snicker to each other, never quite realizing that they were the targets of every other marketing department in Oceania.

And whether it was a marketing department or not, at least half of the consumers slaving away in the corporate farms of the Capitalist (whose portrait hung atop every entrance, decorated in chains and biting happily into a leg of turkey and giving a thumbs-up) were called "managers". Like their predecessors on the assembly line, these persons accomplished no real work themselves but spent most of their day talking to each other about the work that others had done, or that they would yet blackmail them into doing. These persons dressed themselves in roughly the same style of outfit and had similar haircuts and accessories, so that like soldiers in an army all vestiges of personality and identity were dim and transparent. Much of the manager's day was spent worrying about organizational charts and titles and who was a vassal and to whom he owned allegiance. He could not understand why when he went home, emotionally exhausted, he felt no satisfaction in day poorly spent.

But as I said, for a time most of the parties involved were content. The consumers endorsed the notion that the person who didn't need anyone was the stronger, the Holy Man enjoyed austere and superficial respect and devotion, and the Politician sat above them all like a king smiling and ogling and trying to stretch his smile a little more. Of course, the Capitalist was there, too, in the background as it were, and things were pretty good for him, as I think I've described, although not as good as they always had been, and that's why I didn't mention him in that jolly list; for the Capitalist, despite his good fortune, did not count himself either happy or lucky.

How much of what I am going to tell you came to pass as the inevitable result of human nature and how much through choice? An interesting question, and I cannot answer it.

At any rate, the more the consumer wanted, the more expensive the products became that the Capitalist continually dangled in front of his eyes, and the more Money he was forced to earn. Eventually, not only one, but both parents had to turn themselves over to the clutches of the Capitalist – even though in his many speeches the Politician was wont to claim that the consumers were richer now than they had ever been before. Their children never saw them, and when they did a vile mixture of guilt, stress, and exhaustion created a fertile ground for tumult. But, well, everyone agreed that products had to be bought and consumed. The Capitalist got the Politician to pass laws that allowed him to ruthlessly collect what was owed to him, so that although the Politician was also able to loudly declare that they all lived in a free society, the consumers lived steeped in permanent debt. Theirs was a quiet and simmering fear that never quite let up. But it was the consumer's dream that one day he himself would sit in a privileged position over other consumers in similar situations, and then there would be ample opportunity for payback. I imagine that thought alone kept a lot of them on their feet.

In fact, the Capitalist achieved this all so subtlety that the consumers never once blamed him, but heaped all their scorn and contempt upon the Politician. Which was an easy enough victory to accomplish, seeing as the Politician lent himself so readily to ridicule. You see, the Capitalist kept pointing to his homemade science and reminded them all that the only reason they had these wonderful gadgets is because of the incentive of profit that rewarded the bravest, the most resourceful – clearly, in a word, the best people, who applied their talents in what was really the only worthy public arena left to them. With this thinking the consumers concurred, partly because of the propaganda, partly because they had grown so spiritually depraved that they happily rejected their social responsibilities. Anyway, such thinking reflected their lives at the office. Misery loves company.

You see, the consumers had lost much of the knowledge and wisdom that a few thousand years before had been plain to many. The consumers abandoned the present and fancied the future; the consumers refused to recognize that many of the forces that shaped their lives lay beyond their control; the consumers cared too much about what other consumers thought of them. That is probably why they were so easy to manipulate. Part of this was the fault of the Holy Man, who liked to have it both ways (you are not responsible at all, he told his listeners on some days, and on others it was: you are responsible for everything). But the Politician was by far the Capitalist's greatest cheerleader. He felt that the Capitalist was a way of life. He openly condoned the belief that the profit justified the means. Which is ironic, because the Politician was also the only bulwark between the Capitalist and the certain destruction he would have faced had he challenged the consumers as he intended before they had been properly conditioned. The Capitalist never knew how lucky he was that he had to contend for so long with the private obstructions of the Politician. Anyway, society – a notion which I think I've described already – began to dissolve. It was because of this notion that the consumers used to greet each other on the streets, or take care of their parents in their old age, or respect spousal relationships, or resist the temptation to terminate someone's employment a few years from his pension.

Alas, the silly consumer. What a disgraceful animal. The chief characteristic of the consumer was that he was selfish. Also, he defined his identity almost entirely in terms of branding and the glossy artifacts of a stunted, mass-produced culture – produced and directed by the Capitalist, of course. A secondary characteristic of the consumer was that he was not at all inclined to exert himself, being used to taking everything he could possibly want pre-packaged off the shelf, whether he paid for it or not. As a result, the consumer had a loud mouth but was in actuality very tame and didn't know how to stand up for anything except perhaps his family. The consumer was very concerned with image and didn't care much for substance. This was most particularly the case with his opinions, the range of which were dictated to him by the Capitalist's propaganda networks in between the endless incantations of slogans. There were only a few accepted opinions, but the consumers took great pride in the variety of ways they could dress them up, or in the cleverness of the delivery as they rehashed them to their friends. They all thought they were being original, and the Politician loudly assured them that they lived in a society where everyone was free to express himself.

So there you have it. In the end, in the part of the world that by conquest of free trade agreements was quickly congealing into Oceania, the unsatisfied husks of human beings were walking past each other without taking notice except perhaps to steal a glance here and there (for sex, too, eventually was to become a commodity, something to be bought and sold and coldly discarded when it wasn't needed any more, to lie idle somewhere unseen until it was called for again), talking loudly on whatever communication devices were in vogue at the time, bumping into one another by accident and just walking away, as if another person were a pole, or a pile or garbage. All saying pretty much the same things with the same limited vocabularies and vomiting up those same prepackaged laughs and trying to get one up on his best friend.

Yes, the consumers were always talking. They had a lot to say about everything, especially those things they knew the least about or had heard from somebody else. Because as every consumer knew, it was much more fun to embellish than to actually spend time going after the truth. Which was a cumbersome process anyway and seemed to require genuine interest. From a distance the consumers tried to act like each other, to conform to the same pre-approved archetypes they observed on their social networks, so that even though in theory they celebrated their individuality, in actuality they were just cattle, like the Communist had openly declared for himself. And the consumers, despite a vague but permanent feeling of dissatisfaction, honestly believed that they had far better lives than the people in the other, as yet "uncivilized" parts of the world, where they still depended upon one another.

For even if the people had lived in squalor and had suffered from rotting teeth and skin conditions and wore ragged clothes, they had still been people and accepted their own natures as animals. Not so the consumer. The consumer was perfectly groomed – every hair in its place, even in a strong wind – sometimes tattooed, and happily branded himself as a loyal supporter of his favorite corporations. Sometimes these were sports teams, sometimes they were the producers of electronics, sometimes of clothing or footwear. He looked back with disdain upon the days when his ancestors had lived in the country. Great hairy apes, they thought to themselves, who hadn't the proper sense to have their sweat glands removed or that operation to eliminate flatulence. The consumer did not accept his humanity and was uncomfortable on those scant occasions when he was confronted with it.

Perhaps I have judged the consumer harshly. After all, he was under someone else's influence. But this question of responsibility, it plagues me. If this was our destiny, if from the very beginning this had been the only way, then I should not complain, for it must merely have been a step in the Universe's development. But if it was not... Well, let me say this about the consumer: time dragged on for him, during which he was constantly tossed about and buffeted by the contradiction between what his heart was telling him and the realities of his life. Before he knew it he was elderly and had not many years left, and yet he had the vague but unshakable sense that he hadn't actually lived. And then the consumer died.

The Capitalist belched heartily. Tiny flecks of meat sprayed from his mouth, pummeling the filthy surface of the table in front of him like ragged comets striking a devastated moon. A fat hand reminiscent of a bundle of sausages jiggled the sack of flesh still held together by a loose packet of unidentifiable grey fur. "Well, it's a damned waste, and that's always a shame when Money's in question." The Capitalist was fatter than natural human proportion should ever have allowed. His sturdy silver chair had been replaced several times until now he took up one whole side of the table. When he wasn't sitting in it (which was rare) one would have mistaken it for an ugly park bench, albeit one made of reinforced steel. In fact, the Capitalist had taken up permanent residence in the room with the table and the chairs inside the great grey building with the gates and the guards. He never left. Perhaps he feared he would no longer fit through the opening. Perhaps he knew better. Anyway, the Capitalist was loath to be away from the seat of his power and did not miss fresh air or a change of scenery or the warmth of the sun or a glimpse of green. Alright, perhaps a little, but it was never enough to overcome his more civilized desires.

The Politician and the Holy Man were crowded together on the other side. The Politician hadn't changed much over the decades except that his smile was even wider, his hair even greasier and even more perfectly sculpted, his clothes still conservative, but even finer and more sumptuous. Of course, he was a great deal richer these days, perhaps not as rich as he was wont to expect in ages gone by, but certainly he had nothing to complain about. He had a steady stream of income now provided by the Capitalist, something he had never known before. The security of that income had softened the Politician even as it increased his isolation from reality.

At the moment, the Politician was engaged in a seemingly perpetual attempt to keep a rocking boat from sinking. Calmly, almost simply, he was speaking to the Capitalist, as if he were addressing a strong but errant child whose heart was basically in the right place. "Well, I don't see how you will get the workers you need if we don't educate them. Some of what you do requires specific skills, does it not?" If the Politician had had glasses he would have peered patiently over them at the Capitalist. He had to settle with twisting a lock of hair between his forefingers.

"I'm not saying they shouldn't be trained for their life's work!" exclaimed the Capitalist, waving his arms emphatically and wiping his dripping face with a handkerchief. He brought the packet of fur to his face and ripped out a sizable chunk of flesh with a gaping maw. Flinging his arms wide, bits of soft grey fur were left spinning stupidly in the air, zigzagging their way carelessly towards the ground. "Naturally I need trained workers! Some of them, that is. But I don't see why they have to learn all this other stuff. It takes too long and it's free which means we have to pay for it. Not to mention the fact that when they are sitting in those silly classrooms, it's time that they aren't spending in my offices!" He spoke while he was chewing, which means he was spitting. It's part of the reason why the Politician and the Holy Man sat so far away. That, and the smell, of course.

The Politician coughed uncomfortably. The consumers, he knew, had come to expect a general education because he had promised it as part of the social contract introduced during the time of the Communist. "The consumers want their children to go to school."

"Bullshit," belched the Capitalist and ripped another bite out of the packet of fur. "No one likes to go to school. Believe me, they'll all be overjoyed when you make the announcement." The Capitalist shrugged. "Just throw up a few more stadiums and let me set up some more teams – whatever sports happen to be in fashion, you know. We'll let them in for free but we'd have to sell the snacks and articles of clothing and such, and –"

"Let them in for free?" The Politician, as often happened, didn't quite understand. "I thought the whole point –"

"If they are spending their time cheering madly in a stadium or engaged in some useful" – the Capitalist belched again – "and constant labor, they won't have much time to sit around and think, will they? Anyway, they'll love you for it. Much more than they claim to now for this so-called education."

"Education is the light that illuminates the mind," hissed the Holy Man. He, too, looked very much as he always had, except now he wore sunglasses (even indoors) and he had his legs up on the table much more frequently. He rarely spoke these days, and when he did it was softly and in a voice that purred. It was a voice that seemed not to care much one way or the other. If you happened to be speaking to him, you might easily have come away with the impression that behind the screen of darkened glass he was looking up at the ceiling, staring off someplace far away, someplace that made him giggle occasionally and for seemingly no reason at all. The soft, red and white embroidered robes were still magnificent but neglected and fading in some places.

The Capitalist grimaced. "Why do you have to come out and speak such nonsense?"

The Holy Man shrugged.

"Why can't you just say what you mean?"

The Holy Man shrugged again.

The Capitalist turned to the Politician. "Why can't he just say what he means?"

Now it was the Politician's turn to shrug. "He thinks it makes him sound wise. Anyway, the consumers get educated and that's that."

The Capitalist cast an iron glance in the Politician's direction.

The Holy Man, smoothing his robes, giggled. "You don't know what a thorn in my side this whole education business is. These students, they get these strange ideas in their heads. It takes time to beat it out of them."

"They get an education," repeated the Politician resolutely. He squirmed slightly in his chair.

The Capitalist took note. "Ah, excuse me, but weren't you the one who started taking Money away from the universities in the first place?" The man's voice was frothing with sarcasm. "And did anyone complain?"

The Politician's mind raced. Yes, it was true he had started to reduce the quality of education available to everyone. Still, it was there for those who really needed it, he told himself. And the Money was being used for other parts of the social contract. The social contract. In a sudden flash of intuition, he realized it was degrading. "I don't see your point."

"Let's be honest here," said the Capitalist. "An intelligent, free-thinking electorate is not in your best interests. It's certainly not in mine. I'm simply suggesting we finally complete a task started half-assed!"

The Politician felt slightly ill. Everything the Capitalist said was true, but he most certainly didn't put it to himself like that. "They get an education."

"Fine then. But not for free."

The Politician, brushing away his own personal bitterness, considered again. The Capitalist was right, of course. He was simply afraid of the fallout. But it was a proposition he could probably squeeze by the consumers, accompanied by the right propaganda, of course. The Capitalist's news broadcasts could begin to emphasize the luxurious and do-nothing lifestyle of the professional student, sucking off society like a parasite, and cast this image on all students everywhere. Immediately, he saw an array of arguments he could arm himself with. He could claim it was a matter of justice; he could claim that students would value their education the more by it; he could claim that there weren't enough resources to educate everyone, and that therefore only those who deserved it should have access to them first. "Fine, they'll pay."

The Capitalist nodded with satisfaction. "Don't worry," he snorted, "you'll get your cut as always." So, the students would keep streaming out the universities with ideas of their own, but at least their numbers would begin to dwindle and anyway, now he would reap a profit from it. Education had become a legitimate business at last. There would come another time to deal with the remainder of the problem. The Capitalist had learned to bide his time. He took another bite of meat.

"What is that?" purred the Holy Man with disgust. He couldn't hold it back anymore.

"I found it pissing on a tree outside."

"You know," the Politician told him, "some little boy or girl is probably missing that animal right now."

The Capitalist giggled. "I know. That's the best part."

The Politician hurried onward. "The consumers have not been too receptive of our housing plans."

The Capitalist shrugged. "Well, we won't give them any choice."

"I don't see what you mean."

"If they want to keep renting, let them rent." The Capitalist, although he made a hearty profit from the business, didn't like renters. He liked the borrowers. One missed payment and the consumer had nothing, no matter how much he had already sunk into the matter, not to mention all the legal remedies available to the Capitalist to recover his property. The Capitalist would make sure the conditions were such that this happened fairly often. Often enough, in fact, that the consumer could never quite feel independent of his master, despite all the propaganda which assured him otherwise. "We'll just change the zoning laws and limit the number of units available. All the good housing will be for sale. If they want to live in filthy neighborhoods, let them rent." The Capitalist smiled. There was a special place in his heart for the land barons, right next to the insurance barons and the law barons.

The Politician nodded his head and made some notes.

"And as far as the hospitals go –"

But the Politician interrupted him sternly. "Absolutely not. You're grubby hands stay off." The consumers, it seemed, were especially attached to the various devices that had been invented for prolonging and improving their general health. They would not so easily forgive the man who would take them away.

"Nothing for free," the Capitalist rasped, his face twisting in a mass of shifting folds. He was especially incensed by the fact that health care remained out of his grasp. It openly flouted the proposition that he himself was the only tenable road to efficiency and innovation. The idea that someone could be motivated by any reason other than greed made him edgy. But he also imagined that to get his grip on the very blood and bones of his workers would install greater fear in them – and thus greater obedience.

"You have your insurances," the Politician reminded him.

"No one really needs them," the Capitalist whined. "I'm having trouble getting the consumers to take out policies." Then and there the Capitalist resolved that all the most useful technologies would from then on be produced in his laboratories. Yes, of course. It would require a sizable investment up front, but what better excuse with which to arm himself later on when he wanted to reap limitless profits from the newest treatments? With a few broadly written patents, slowly but surely he would take over the new terrain medicine was venturing into and leave the Politician to rot in the old, the realm of surgery with knives and drugs with odious side effects.

He knew that the consumer would gladly waste the most productive time of his life, slaving away for the Capitalist, just to be reassured that he would eventually be cured of degenerative brain disease in his impotent old age when a mere handful of years were left to him. "I'll start with the genes," he said aloud. "Yes, I'll put out patents on runny noses and black hair."

"Excuse me?" It was the Holy Man. He hadn't really been paying much attention, but the sentence jumped out at him.

The Capitalist giggled. He found the irony amusing. "Pathetic little consumers. Nothing more than overdressed peasants is what they are." The Capitalist was surprised to hear both the Holy Man and the Politician chuckle.

"Yes," concurred the Politician, grinning grotesquely as he was wont to do. "Big little peasants with electronic gadgets. Nothing has changed except the gadgets." He threw a glance at the Holy Man.

"Nothing has changed," repeated the Holy Man.

"Fashions come and go my friend, but those ignorant peasants, they remain. Masks, just masks. As they grow bolder we have to speak nicer words to them, I guess, but –"

"Nothing's changed – except now they wear underwear," said the Holy Man, interrupting.

The Capitalist burst out laughing. Now they were all three of them laughing, having a merry old time.

"It's nice to see that you're catching up," the Politician told the Capitalist once they had settled down.

The Capitalist, immensely pleased with himself, grinned and bit into his hunk of flesh.

And in a like manner many such things were decided.

Now, it was about this time that the Politician began to seriously devote his attention to the business of acquiring an empire. It was considered the most time-honored and noble duty of the Politician, although I can't for the life of me imagine why. At any rate, assembling a successful empire was the key to a position of unassailable strength for the Politician, and never before had his prospects seemed so bright. For when the Politician had empire, he was respected and feared by those from whom respect and fear are the most helpful. As he well knew, the seat of the Politician's power was firmly planted in the minds of his subjects and his rivals. Like the Holy Man, his position depended in no small part upon perception. But there was a more insidious reason: war and discord, if the consumers were behind him, provided a suitable mask for suppressing dissent.

Yes, believe it or not, there was such a thing as dissent, although the word has passed from our carefully clipped vocabularies. You see, there once was a time when it was not presumed there was only one valid opinion about any particular matter. In fact, there used to be as many points of view as there were persons to have them. Yes, disagreement sometimes led to strife and conflict, but more often than not human beings were worked out their differences and even learned from each other. This is why it was so important, it was felt, that human beings develop themselves fully and completely, so that by knowing who they were, what strengths and weaknesses they possessed, they were best able to represent their particular points of view when the occasion presented itself. For the Universe had vested itself in each and every one of them, tiny sparks of light that were working towards some greater purpose.

Alas, I am talking over your head, and I apologize. I can see your eyes glazing over, and that isn't an encouraging sign. I must hurry onward.

The Politician, then, decided to act when he did because of the presence and popularity of the Capitalist. Ah, the silly man, like Pompeius Magnus he never realized that he was setting up a dangerous rival. He trusted too much to his own reputation. He did not see how the consumers sighed with delight when the

Capitalist reported how much he had grown in the previous year. He did not understand the subtle jibes constantly made in his direction. For the consumers, even if they acted stupidly, were not actually stupid, and they could see quite clearly what was going on. The only time they ever showed any liking for the Politician was when the Capitalist convinced him to give them largess in the form of tax breaks.

But the consumer's pride in the Capitalist did provide the Politician with one new weapon, and that was nationalism. The consumers seemed to think that their country was a sports team and there was nothing they loved more than to see their country winning. Their love for their material possessions and their envy at the fact that outside their borders there were still people in the world (they came into restless and uncomfortable contact with them whenever the consumers ventured there on vacation) encouraged the Politician to resort to empire as a way to shore up his own sagging position in the Gang of Three. The only condition was that no consumers should be killed. People, now that was a different story, and anyway they were foreigners. As long as the Capitalist's propaganda networks shielded the consumers of Oceania from the human devastation of the Politician's wily ways, they would suffer no discomfort at the hand of their consciences, and happy life could go on as always.

During this time the Politician gave an extraordinary number of speeches. We all know that words mean very little and they also come cheaply, which is why the Politician was so free with them. Standing on the rostra haranguing the consumers, that was what he was best at. Naturally, he never felt compelled to act on anything he promised in his speeches, and now that the consumers' minds were bent from exhaustion and emptiness they weren't apt to take him to task for anything he said or even to bother remembering it. His favorite topic was "freedom", of course. The consumers of Oceania had been born into a strong tradition of "freedom", although the word (for some reason) rang strangely hollow in the mouth. Which is why they craved the speeches of the Politician as they did. They needed to be

The Politics of Consumption

reassured that they possessed this fleeting jewel, the reality of which eluded them.

The Politician pointed out the towering corporate farms that crowded the ever-expanding cities. These, he reminded them, produced the devices and gadgets that provided entertainment and acted as a convenient source of identity. Not far away the imposing goal posts of the nearest stadium stabbed into the air. This, the Politician told them warmly, is where they were provided with free public spectacles of sport and physical prowess. For those who wanted less from their lives, he pointed out the government buildings and the universities and the libraries and the hospitals. But the Politician didn't dwell much on these. Government services, you see, were almost non-existent, since the general feeling was that only the Capitalist could render any service efficiently and anyway, if a service couldn't earn a reliable profit then it wasn't worth having. The universities had become dull bastions of archaic thought, since thinking about anything other than making Money had long since been left to the weaklings of Oceania. All the best minds labored for the Capitalist, waiting up at night ready to do his bidding. And anyway, the costs of attending these universities was so extraordinarily high that few consumers could afford it. And yet, the Politician was rightly able to claim that the universities existed with their doors open. Libraries were solemn graveyards for the aging wardens of the books. Each year they would bury a few more beneath the moldy shelves.

As for the hospitals, well, over the years the Capitalist had taken out patents on gene therapy and the workings of the mind and all the other useful advancements, just as he said he would. The administrators and doctors in these hospitals became the minions of the Capitalist even though officially they worked under the auspices of the Politician. But everyone agreed, the Capitalist had invested so much Money in producing these wonderful new technologies, it was only right that he recouped what he had spent as well as a decent profit on top of it all. According to the law, the Capitalist actually owned the bodies of the persons who ventured into his hospitals, and because he owned them he was entitled to do with them what he wanted. If he needed a gene or an organ he took it without asking and without warning. As it was, the price for access to these technologies was such that only the consumers who played his game got the treatment they required. Because as everyone knew, a consumer's worth was only to be measured by how much Money he had, and a consumer couldn't obtain Money without laying himself first on the altar of the Capitalist. Anyway, it worked out extremely well. Between kidneys and mortgages, the Capitalist was in a position to ensure that no one passed on any wealth or independence to his children.

Yes, freedom. The word sent chills up and down the spines of more than a few persons listening. Yes, some of them received the word with a very specific skepticism, even a sickening dread that brought to mind late night beatings and electric shocks and waterboarding. More than a few knew exactly what kind of freedom they could expect within the confines of Oceania. For the Politician had been busy over the years decreeing laws on behalf of the Gang of Three. Yes, his laws filled books and books and rooms and rooms and archives and archives, and still he made more of them. There were laws on absolutely every subject imaginable and every situation. Yes, the citizens of Oceania were free to obey the laws that had been created to govern every aspect of their lives. Although initially they were rarely applied, the fact was that if any one of the Gang wanted to put anyone away for any amount of time, the laws were there to ensure that every citizen was guilty of something. Yes, there were some in the audience listening who knew exactly what kind of freedom they enjoyed, but they dared not utter any dissenting remarks. The number of prison farms in Oceania was quickly approaching the number of corporate farms, and the Capitalist made quite a profit from them, too, since the labor of the inmates was cheap. And if anyone tried to force the Politician to consider proposals that would correct the situation – to clean up the polluted environment, for instance – the

The Politics of Consumption

Capitalist would shout at the top of his lungs that his profits would suffer and he'd have to kick a whole slew of consumers out of his corporate farms. They consumers knew what that meant. No work meant no food, no more fancy gadgets, and no more health care. So that was usually the end of that.

The Politician always ended his speeches with a long, hypnotic tribute to National Capitalism, a phrase he had coined himself long ago in a slightly different form but had now found useful to recycle. And the consumers, even if they might have grown uncomfortable hearing about "freedom", or had survived the brutal innards of any one of the many prison farms, would suddenly go mad with delight, shouting and clapping their hands and waving flags and generally feeling very good about themselves and Oceania and their Gang of Three. For by now every other land had a Gang of Three as well. They, too, had begun to accrete. But they were poor, backwards barbarians, far behind the shining beacon of progress that was Oceania and her provinces.

Off to the side of the rostra sat the Holy Man, slouching in his chair with his legs thrown wide. Remember him? His splendid robes were faded and wrinkled, and he had grown a beard again. Except this time it was hardly impressive. Long, wiry threads that cupped his chin and captured odors and gave something else to look at besides the empty expression behind his eyes. He hardly moved, he hardly spoke, but there he was, he was always there, watching without seeming to care. Perhaps you noticed how the Holy Man was not himself. Perhaps you noticed how silent and inattentive he was at the meetings of the Gang of Three. The Capitalist had joked now and then through the vidscreens about removing him from the Gang altogether, but the Politician hadn't laughed. He no longer savored the idea of being alone with the Capitalist inside the building with the gates and the guards. The Holy Man had only looked blankly between the Politician and the vidscreens and hummed some ancient reggae tune, as if it were all the same to him.

But it wasn't all the same to him, and that's why he had crawled into himself. The Holy Man was acutely absorbed in his relationship with the Universe, or he had been once. Now he couldn't understand why it was allowing him to be slowly erased. Oh, he didn't believe anymore that there was this all-powerful entity looking down loading the dice. That was, of course, a silly notion. But there was a plan nonetheless, for the machinery was there, that was plain. The workings of the Universe were subtlety and vastly complex, light years beyond the scope of his imagination he knew now, and yet all that happened everywhere across suns and galaxies was geared in the same direction. The direction was there and he knew there was no point pretending we had any control over it or that it even mattered if we knew where it was going. We were simply a part of it, and merely by living.

Which is why he couldn't stand that the Capitalist was winning out over the rest of them.

He had wrestled first with the notion that because there were no gods to appease, because there was no judgment, that it naturally followed it was pointless to philosophize and to speculate over the nature of being human. After all, the myth behind his power relied entirely upon this assumption. But after some time he decided that it was not so, and he thought back through the centuries to the time when he had stressed to those who would listen that a human being must learn to confront the ego in himself if he is ever to achieve any enduring peace, that he must recognize where his sphere of action lies and accept it. The present is all we have; the past is a ghost and the future may never come.

There was a flutter near his head. A shadow fell over him and darkened his vision. Far back in his mind the image was projected – what was it? Familiar, yes, vague shadows standing before a tribunal. Someone was on trial. Yes, there was the faint, burnt smell of judgment hanging in the air. What was it? Where was it? How long ago? He had been there. He stood listening. To whom?

The Politics of Consumption

As yes, to that man there, pacing in front of the tribunal, gesticulating, but not wildly, no. With extreme precision and vast success. Oh, he remembered him now. How he had hated him. Self-righteous bastard. He had got what was coming to him. What was he saying? No, not again, he didn't want to hear that nagging voice again, filled with self-importance. The people remained shadows, black outlines framed against the monstrosity of time itself, but the voice, that voice...

Marcus Tullius, giving a speech, of course. Insisting that he is his own master, that he will not be intimidated, that he can control his passions and does not seek wealth. Insisting on his moral *integrity*.

The Holy Man shook his head. What was happening to him? The wings flapping about his head withdrew for a moment.

Yes, he was withdrawn. Withdrawn into himself, engaged in a painful process of recognition and acceptance. Ah, how that only made him think even more of long ago. Yes, back in the day when he knew how important it was to recognize what was already a fact and then to accept it as a fact. For there was no point in railing against what already was, nor in pretending to oneself childishly that it was not so.

Ah, the wings again, fluttering near his ears, and another image. It was an old man, not entirely unlike himself, and yet very much so. He was careworn, too, but seemed to holding up much better than the Holy Man. Hunched over a writing tablet in the dim light of an oil lamp. It was cold, very cold, and there were barbarians outside. Yes, he knew this man. He remembered him well.

What was he writing? Ah, he needed to see. He peered carefully over the shoulder of the living shade, holding his breath. It was important...

Marcus Aurelius, referring to his adoptive father and the lessons he learned from him: wisely knowing when to insist and when to desist in an argument, not to pay much attention to flattery, and perhaps most important of all, not to be ashamed of the artifacts of luxury, but not to dwell on them when they are unavailable.

The Holy Man frowned. The Universe paused. The stars seemed to be holding their breath. The constellation of Orion looked expectantly down. The Holy Man knew he had arrived at a momentous crossroads. It was a second chance. The phrase echoed in his head.

A second chance? At what? The Holy Man thought back.

Yes, long ago – ages ago, in fact – when the Holy Man and the Politician sat in state in quite a different empire, in a different part of the world even, he had recognized a critical defect in the social fabric, just as he had now. Yes, it was called "pleasure". He had seen first hand what happened when human beings gave themselves entirely to it. It was slavery of a different kind, but slavery nonetheless. Self-discipline fell away. Human beings ceased to perform the work of human beings. There was chaos and pain, ah, such pain. Because pleasure often had to be ripped away from others. Ah, yes, so he had devised a solution then, one that had bought a new lease on civilization. Pleasure, he had eventually decreed, must be done away with entirely. Especially sexual pleasure.

What a sad turn of events. Sad, because for humankind it meant that an important aspect of life and a strong social cement was turned into a hideously misunderstood demon that came occasionally to torment the bitter and frustrated persons the Holy Man eventually came to approve of. These men and women, proud and vain, extolled the virtues of war and murder, confounding them with bravery and duty, and condemned love and affection in all except its most ceremonious forms.

Above him, Orion blinked. If they could, the stars would have spoken to him.

Just because a thing can be abused, is it wise to do away with it entirely?

The Holy Man shook his head determinedly. And then he had it.

Orion cocked his head remorsefully. The stars twinkled. The Universe shrugged and moved on.

The Holy Man decided that there was indeed a place for him in the Gang of Three, and if he was to secure it he must act and he must act quickly. He saw clearly where his sphere of action lay. He recognized that too much lay outside his control. But he also saw that the medical technology of the Capitalist allowed him – for the first time in the history of humanity – to alter the borders between what must merely happen and what he could actually do about it. The consumers belonged to the Capitalist, yes, but it was a mistake. Nature could be trusted to arrive at the general formula, but it would require the tastes and understanding of an artist to polish off the work.

If pleasure was so steeped in the nature of being human that to deprive them of it immersed them in great, inner turmoil, then he would simply remove it from their nature altogether. The imperfect would become the perfect, the impure would be purified. And the consumers would love him for it, for he would remove at long last the greatest source of internal friction they had ever known.

Yes, with some creative restructuring of their genetic makeup, the consumers would be his. And the Capitalist, he could be dealt with in such a way that he wouldn't recognize the threat until it was too late.

For the first time in years, sitting to one side of the rostra while the Politician was busy haranguing the people, the Holy Man grinned. It was an unsettling sight if you had cared to look. When he was invited by the Politician for the customary afterparty, he refused. The Politician was taken aback. The Holy Man hadn't missed an afterparty and all of the wonderful mind-altering drugs since as far back as any of them could remember.

The possibilities were endless, he realized after some small contemplation. Because really, now that the logical structure of the human mind was understood, now that they could determine exactly what comprises a decision and the role of the will in formulating them and how their implementation changed depending upon perspective and where emotions find their roots and how they affect decisions and what are the various layers of thought and how language affects consciousness and how observation and experience are filtered and subsequently translated into knowledge and what the various classes of knowledge are and how it is actually stored and retrieved and lost even – because the scientists claimed to understand all these things, he realized that there was simply no point in trusting any longer to a consumer's own self-restraint. No, consumers needed to be protected from themselves, and more importantly, the consumer's activities should be wholly directed in the interests of those who knew better, and the best way to accomplish this lofty goal would be to cut away all sense of independence and self-determination from the brain itself. Let them act in a very predictable and reliable way. With he himself holding the strings, of course, as it was always meant to be. Fate, destiny: these concepts would disappear for the Holy Man, yes, but they would become the order of the day for those slinking consumers out there, dull-witted and obtuse. Uneducated, sickly, ignorant even; slightly confused, easily distracted, entirely colorless. An eternal question troubled their faces day and night, but very few of them were able to think clearly enough to formulate it.

The Holy Man needed, of course, access to the Capitalist's scientists, so when he had stopped frothing at the mouth and had straightened up his cumbersome hat and wiped away the grime that had collected on his sunglasses, he hobbled over to the building with the gates and the guards. The Holy Man was not heading for the room with the table and the chairs. The table and the chairs were no longer in it, for there was no longer space for anything other than the Capitalist's undulating mass of flesh, kilograms and kilograms upon kilograms of flowing fat like lava where hardly a blood vessel could find its way. The room had been expanded. A new ventilation system had been added, too, because like a waking volcano the Capitalist was constantly emitting a variety of noxious gases, poisonous to most life forms, including himself.

The Holy Man found the Politician in the Observation Room, as they called it, speaking hastily into the huge, liquid wall monitor that comprised an entire side of the room. The Capitalist's fat, sagging face towered over them, his pasty, unhealthy looking skin oozing some combination of urine and oil and preservatives. His mouth opened and closed. He was in the process of chewing something. A huge, cavernous mouth that threatened to suck them all inside. The Holy Man took an instinctive step backwards. The Capitalist's breathing, too, was all around them. High quality speakers were positioned inside the armrests of the couches where no one dared to sit. Everyone stood when addressing the Capitalist. Laborious, exhausted, his lungs were on the verge of collapse. It was a fact that the man got most of his oxygen through artificial means, but the brain wouldn't give up the habit it had acquired over millions of years.

In fact, much of the Capitalist's time these days was spent perfecting small devices that could act as remote extensions of his life and limbs. Not robots, not yet, they didn't know how to wire their command centers directly into his brain, but simple sensors hanging in the streets or at other key locations throughout Oceania. Some of them he could control with switches and knobs, turning and twisting and zooming and listening and watching. Now that he was trapped inside that little room from which all power was exercised, he began to be seized by bouts of paranoia. He had heard of all-powerful men and women, deep inside fortresses of respite from which they never emerged, blinded by their advisors and colleagues and guilefully manipulated. Such lives tended to end badly. And the technology available was remarkable. The more the consumers sacrificed their own, personal happiness for his profit, the more they worked and competed with each other for petty rewards, the more interesting and provocative became the personal situation of the Capitalist.

"It's going to be extremely difficult convincing anyone of that," the Politician was telling the Capitalist doubtfully.

"Don't spit problems back at me. I want solutions!"

"Of course you do. But you see, these are your laws, all this about private property. We can't simply install electronic billboards in people's living rooms!"

The Capitalist was silent for a moment. He grumbled something along the lines of, "Do I have to do everything myself?" and then suddenly there rang out a voice neither of them had heard clearly in quite some time.

"Consumers can own land, but if I recall correctly, no one can own space." It was the Holy Man who spoke. The Politician whirled about in surprise, his lips parted, his head bobbing uncertainly.

The Capitalist chuckled, a difficult series of sounds to describe. "We've finished sulking, have we?" The vidscreen was sprayed with flecks of garbage.

The Holy Man shrugged and looked at the Politician.

"What do you mean, space? Are you saying – Ah, I see what you are saying." The Politician turned again to the Capitalist. He pursed his lips in thought. "Actually, we could probably justify it legally. As long as the billboards don't come in contact with the floor, I think we'll be on reasonably solid ground. After all, that's why we've got lawyers."

"Just make sure they don't interfere with the gambling machines," barked the Capitalist, ejecting at the same moment from his putrid feeding hole a rather large chunk of foul, grey material. It stuck insistently to the other side of the vidscreen before it was slowly pulled downwards, leaving a hefty smear to mark its trail.

The Politician coughed uncomfortably. "You'll drop the appropriate hints in the news?"

The Capitalist ignored him. He was eyeing the Holy Man with obvious distrust. "What do you want?"

"Scientists," answered the Holy Man.

"Scientists? What for?"

"I'm going to purify the consumers."

The Politician looked up aghast. "Purify?" He hadn't heard the Holy Man use that word in a long time. It brought back memories of the day the Holy Man had made him stand in the snow outside his castle all night long and beg.

"Yes."

The Capitalist gurgled. Most of his plans at the moment involved making the most of the free trade agreements he had got the Politician to sign. Now he had offices everywhere, towering skyscrapers and vast factories, and with each passing day the consumers of Oceania fell more and more under a single umbrella. He didn't see how this purification business would get in the way. Because really, he didn't care what kind of consumers they were as long as they were the kind who consumed, and avidly. "Fine."

"Fine?" The Politician whirled around. "Don't you see – Can't you – No, of course you can't." He turned back to the Holy Man in desperation. But that one was already gone.

Of course, in the end the scientists proved to know a lot less about the mechanics of the human mind than they had claimed. Most of their attempts to interfere with the great motivators of the human mind – emotions – were disastrous. As it turned out, a mind is actually quite a vast and complex system, and it is resting on a very precipitous balance, as it were. All the contributing parts are very closely interdependent, and sometimes what seemed to be an insignificant, direct association with one actually turned out to be an enormous, indirect association with some other. At any rate, the first modified human beings they produced were incredibly insane, some torturously, so that as soon as they had been turned on they tore out their tongues and eyes, and others pathologically, bent on tearing out the tongues and eyes of their initiators. So very quickly it became apparent that the Holy Man wasn't going to produce the perfectly obedient and self-effacing consumer after all. Still, they were able to meet with some successes. In the end, despite the goals he had originally set for himself, the Holy Man was pleased with his new creation.

He arranged with the Capitalist the use of some of the most prime real estate in the heart of Oceania for the coming out party. There were several locations, actually, all wired together. Huge, undulating vidscreens dominated the walls, displaying an array of vague and shifting pyrotechnic three-dimensional dance patterns into which the consumers could actually leap. Laser beams like vast glowing appendages stabbed through the dank, smoky air and tickled the ceiling. The music was not exactly pleasant, at least not to my taste, but the consumers who were present seemed to enjoy it. It wasn't really music that was listened to but felt rather and was promulgated by huge bass generators hidden under the floor. The deadened bodies gyrating helplessly on the balconies and the stage and main hall were all responding to vibrations that descended upon them out of the smoke and the air, or leaped up at them from the roots of their feet.

There was quite a selection of party drugs, of course. The Capitalist made a lot of Money from this traffic, and even more from the fact that it was illegal. Not only was it a handy excuse whenever he wanted to have someone picked up, but he derived almost as much Money from the effort expended on putting a stop to it. Weapons, armor, prisons, personnel: they were only the spear tips of a much larger web of industries. And it had provided the Capitalist with a convenient excuse to do something he had never dared before: build his own army and police forces, loyal to no one but their cherished medical benefits and some of the choicest parcels of real estate, all of which they knew they had only the Capitalist to thank for. The Capitalist's doctors kept up the propaganda that there were no substantial side effects to the use of these various synthetic substances, and the consumers were only too happy to hear it. For the consumer had come to regard happiness and contentment as something that could be predictably switched on and off, as opposed to a state of mind that occurred naturally and in tune with his own personal relationship with the Universe. Indeed, the only time the consumer ever felt calm and relaxed and at peace with himself was after he had swallowed some pill or dropped some liquid into his eye and immersed himself in one of these glowing afterparties. Occasionally there were fights, or someone would trip and hurtle hundreds of meters to his death, but no one was bothered. Those standing by would look on and smile, perhaps even tap a friend's shoulder and laugh.

In the center of the vast dance halls were holographic consoles. It was from these consoles that the Holy Man planned to stage the official unveiling. No, the Holy Man wouldn't actually be present in person. There were too many troublemakers and wizened old men hiding away in what was left of the universities who fervently resisted the machinations of the Holy Man, and despite his best efforts, no one could stamp out the pestilence once and for all. The event was publicized as open to everyone, but in fact every consumer present had been carefully screened beforehand.

When the great moment finally arrived, the consumers stopped gyrating. The holographic consoles flickered and came to life. Suddenly, in the middle of the room, was the unblemished image of the Holy Man standing before what appeared to be a couch covered in a white sheet. Clearly, someone was seated on that couch, hidden by the sheet. Whoever it was was very still. No fanfare or herald was necessary to grab the consumers' attention. Eyes were fastened in an instant to that couch, to whomever was content to be sitting under that sheet, perfectly still, unashamed, unperturbed.

Well, there is no need to describe any more of that scene, disconcerting enough as it was. The Holy Man had, in fact, provided for fanfare, because he was a great deal excited himself. You see, he imagined he had found a replacement for his audience, and even through their drug induced stupor the consumers couldn't help but sense it. They stood in silence listening to him, the cavernous vibrations of the music still landing in sonic booms all around. The Holy Man spoke vigorously, gesticulating forcefully, and the expression on his face, though stern, was sincere. And yet, the consumers knew that as real as he seemed, if they had tried to touch the Holy Man their hands would have gone right through. The Politician, watching from the building with the gates and the guards, shook his head and couldn't understand why the Holy Man hadn't asked for help. There were ways of doing things, ways sanctioned by time and experience. But the Holy Man didn't believe in masks of that kind. He believed in his madness, he was proud of it, and that's why he didn't try and hide it from anyone.

The new consumer had no genitals. All capacity for pleasure had been cut away. "Because," the Holy Man spat at them from the holographic consoles, "sex is dirty and you all know it." Sex, the Holy Man concluded, was a word that must be removed from the dictionary. All sense of feeling, in fact, had been deadened in the new consumer except for fear and pain. Pain, felt the Holy Man, was especially useful, and fear was the only reliable way to restrain troublemakers. After all, the new consumer constituted only a part of what he had wanted to accomplish. The same applied to taste (food should be a white gruel with the consistency of runny eggs) and to sound (the new consumer encountered music as a great mass of grating noise which needed to be extinguished as quickly as possible). The new consumer wasn't much for small-talk but preferred instead to pronounce absurdly grand and sweeping statements intended to convince everyone of some overwhelming truth. A boldness unrestrained by self-doubt intimidated the consumer, who felt tiny and worthless in the presence of his would-be replacement. It was difficult for the consumer to come to terms with this new creature, for the new consumer, believing itself somehow superior, did not fraternize with him. If it wasn't on some holy mission or working in a factory it would sit quietly in the corner talking to its peers and looking about with eyes full of judgment and await further orders, or perhaps perform some other innocuous activity approved of by the Holy Man, such as sitting relentlessly by its life partner and knitting. The new consumer, however, was extremely and conservatively opinionated, and after making a decision would carry out its consequences without the slightest remorse or compassion. Children who transgressed were often strangled and their bodies displayed to their siblings as a warning.

The consumers, for their part, were willing to accept that sex should be forbidden (for they had long since shunned loving one another, as they had found over the years that these bonds only interfered with one's career), but aside from that one point they were shocked and dismayed by these little, frightening demigods. The Politician noticed it. The Capitalist noticed it. He was the most angry of all. Because when the consumers were upset, they worked less efficiently. Fine, the new consumers were far more efficient, but there simply weren't enough of them, and production couldn't meet demand for some time. The Holy Man, however, believed he had embarked upon a Great Leap Forward. He was waiting, it seemed, for some special and secret message or event that would trigger a great revolution. A revolution whose ultimate accomplishment would be to sweep him into absolute power, Oceania's Champion, its Fountain of Strength.

Whatever the fabulous names and titles were which the Holy Man dreamed up for himself for future historians, the truth is that he became highly unpopular with the consumers, and this was a time when the fact still mattered. I suspect he might have suffered far worse than he already had were it not for the Great War which struck at about this time. And just in time! For as it turned out the new consumers were much better suited to a life of soldiery than ordinary civilian life.

What happened then was this: in a far away land on the border of what was quickly becoming Eurasia and Eastasia, there was a Holy Man equally as fanatical and stubborn as our own. A long time before the two had contracted a feud, and for some reason or another could never see eye to eye. For geographical and cultural reasons the two rarely came into contact. Which, of course, only allowed their feud to settle in over the centuries and take on the manner of habit. By the time of the Great War no one could even remember what they were angry with each other about, least of all the two Holy Men. But it hardly mattered. Everything, naturally, was at stake.

Alas, our story now falls upon the sorry topic war. Fortunately, I need not describe it in too great detail, for it is a phenomenon very familiar to us today. And need I mention how much everyone loves war? Perhaps so. Because even if we workers know why we cheer when we see images beamed down from satellites of our suicide battalion blowing up skyscrapers and factories in Eurasia or Eastasia, or why our blood begins to simmer when we are called down into our shelters or the corporate farm where our brother or sister worked was brought down by an enemy, still, I know it and you know it, everyone loves to talk about war, to praise it, to gorge himself with heady visions of a merciless victory. For what better arena is there for bravery? Certainly not the Capitalist's corporate farms.

The aging propaganda of the Capitalist to the contrary had, of course, long since been discarded, for what choice did one have other than to be a slave? For by now, every sphere imaginable of human activity had been taken over by the Capitalist and averaged out into a very plain and lusterless mediocrity, the artifacts of which were entirely under his control. There we just do as we are told, for fifteen hours a day one after the other.

What better escape from the quiet pain and boredom of our lives than war? Savage beasts are we, not this civilized breed!

Yes, yes, war was certainly nothing new. But the Great War was different from all those that preceded it. It was the first of its kind, the predecessor to today's endless, monotonous litany of destruction. This was not the kind of petty war that the Politician and the Holy Man used to engage in in times past, the kind of war that you would shake your head and laugh at if I even suggested it to you. No, those wars had a loose set of rules and were fought by specially trained people called soldiers who made up fluid formations called armies. In those days, the butchery of war was restricted to these so-called armies, although even in the waning days of the tradition the earth's population had swelled to such an extent that large empty spaces for them to fight in became harder and harder to find. Such wars had cost millions of lives in their time, casualty figures for a few days in ours, and yet everyone took them quite seriously.

Okay, enough about war. When the Holy Man convened a meeting of the Gang of Three in the Observation Room and demanded a reprisal against his foreign competitor, both the Capitalist on the vidscreen and the Politician were enthusiastic. The Politician rubbed his hands together and prepared to make speeches. He would once again expound upon the moral superiority of National Capitalism, a favorite topic. But it was nevertheless disconcerting to hear that his counterpart in a place far away was doing much the same thing, claiming National Capitalism for himself and his Capitalist's workers, although modifying some of the finer details (in so far as there were any) to suit his own needs. But no one was more pleased than the Capitalist, who, surveying the situation, began to formulate a plan, a very nefarious plan indeed. One idea immediately sprang to mind. Smiling, extending a hand, the Capitalist was able to make the Politician a very special offer before he ran off to stir up the enthusiasm of the workers, an offer which he in his haste was only too glad to accept.

You are a busy man, the Politician was told. Let me ease your burden as you embark on this momentous task of yours. Let me bother with the collection of your taxes, your revenues, your booty. I'll simply deliver a dependable sum to you on a regular basis. On the condition that anything I collect above and beyond your requirements I may keep for myself.

There was something else. Everyone carried out missions, natural humans and genetically engineered alike. But the units of the genetically engineered were regularly compromised by the enemy, a fact which the Capitalist arranged himself. You see, although he never said it he presented himself as the one person who would extirpate the Holy Man's pessimistic folly. By doing so he not only gained a great deal of popularity for himself, but he also hardened the workers' bitterness towards the Holy Man.

Anyway, after the Politician had made his initial speeches to the workers, they had expected to be carted away to the battlefront. Alas, it never happened. That's what made this new kind of war so special; the workers themselves were the targets and the battlefield was all around them. They stood on the battlefield while they labored in factories and they stood on it at home mesmerized before the Capitalist's electronic billboards and their children tread on it every day when they went for their life training. Battles and the maneuvering and supplying of armies were cumbersome and no longer achieved results. Everyone knew that the key to victory was industrial production. Everyone knew that the key to keeping your enemy down after the war was to ruin the infrastructure of his economy. That's why this was the first war conducted almost exclusively by the Capitalist who, if I may remind you, had already built up his own armed forces. Oh, sure, there were some dissidents who claimed that this turn of events was alarming, but under the cover of the state of emergency they were quietly picked up, brought around the back of some building, and shot as terrorists. The word, it seems, has many applications. At any rate, it is a fact that enemy workers who managed to infiltrate into Oceania and blow themselves and some factory to bits were reviled as terrorists and thugs, but those brave workers of Oceania (both the traditional and the new) who did the same in Eastasia were considered heroes. You see, the bullshit that had kept the Gang of Three in power for so long was finally nearing its natural conclusion. And the workers had grown so used to swallowing artful rationalizations rather than exercising their own mental prowess that they could not help but agree: anyone labeled by the Capitalist and paraded on his media networks was most certainly a terrorist and should be dealt with accordingly.

So, while the Politician was busy giving speeches and the Holy Man organizing ostentatious and brutal displays in the public stadiums of captured enemy workers, the Capitalist was making some very quiet but important changes to what remained of the social fabric. Last minute adjustments, as it were. And he had the finest excuse imaginable: there was a war on. Dissidents were terrorists. So, while anyone awake enough was left chewing on his own objections, the universities and the hospitals were closed.

Not to everyone, to be sure. The Capitalist looked across the whole of Oceania and he saw one huge, sprawling city with dirty, grit-laden air that accumulated on surfaces and not a single public park or zoo or any other cornered bit of nature for that matter, a world choked with workers, and he realized that it was probably wisest to allow a very small number of closely watched individuals to retain a certain amount of awareness and choice. His eye settled upon the most obsequious of the manager-types. These he called directors. But since they were so few in number it is hardly worth mentioning them.

Next, he closed almost all the shops and stores, the very center of the nexus of greed that had provided the means for his ascent to power. He even went so far as to send someone around to collect all the entertaining junk for centuries he had pawned off on the workers. After all, there was a war on, and raw materials were priced at a premium. Surprising, is it? Not really, not when you realize that the trinkets had served their purpose. For it was no longer the Capitalist's goal to keep score in currency. He simply wanted to possess all the power and live in great opulence and eat food grown in real soil or taken from the carcasses of animals that had actually lived, knowing full well that no one else in the whole world could do the same. The workers, as you can imagine, were greatly distressed at the loss of their toys, but there was a war on. And anyway, the Capitalist convinced the Holy Man to put on more frequent and more bloody spectacles in the public arenas. At these spectacles the drugs and the food (both entirely synthetic) were freely available. The workers were pleased and considered the Capitalist exceptionally gracious to be providing these perks in a time of such scarcity. I have even heard that the Holy Man staged full scale battles among the prisoners in a variety of settings, even going so far as to dig an artificial lake and provide war vessels such as they had in ancient times. The workers greatly enjoyed these ostentatious displays, and to the Holy Man's growing frustration the Capitalist was able to secure most of their gratitude.

There were other changes, too. Pay was drastically reduced. Weekends disappeared. Also, there were new rules about the use of Money. It became illegal on pain of death to possess hard currency. Henceforth, all monetary transactions were to be electronic. And it became illegal for any worker to carry any portion of his salary into the next pay period unspent. This crime was called hoarding and was also punishable by death. The Capitalist, too, drawing from his experience wiring himself to the rest of the world, altered the billboards in his workers' homes so they no longer showed advertisements but whatever broadcasts he chose to beam to them, instructional or otherwise, and fixed it so that he could look out through them. There was, after all, a war on. Sacrifices had to be made, and hiding behind even the friendliest face was a potential terrorist.

Now, everyone loves a good old war. Unless, of course, you happen to be losing, in which case it becomes a very unpopular thing indeed. And there it was: more bombs going off in Oceania every day, more disruption and destruction. These were accompanied by outbreaks of devastating disease, visiting a quick but horrible death upon millions. It cost far more resources to repair what had been vaporized or destroyed and to find replacements for the workers than it did to do the same in far away places. Naturally, the workers' ire turned against the Holy Man. After all, it was his war. And the Capitalist, he did nothing to counter these notions. In fact, he encouraged them.

The Politics of Consumption

The Holy Man, realizing he was cornered, tried to fight back, but he had no leverage with the workers.

In the end, the Capitalist led him down a wide avenue in one of the tax farming districts on some pretext or another. I think the Holy Man believed they were trying to come to some agreement about how best to end the war. The Capitalist was represented by a clunky but functional robot. Through such devices the Capitalist was now able to interact directly with the world outside. He saw through its dim eyes; he heard the audio waves it encountered; it mimicked the words he spoke. At a whim he could flit from the one to the other, anywhere in Oceania that he chose. Little did the Holy Man know that just hours before the Capitalist had inflamed a crowd of workers with stories of the Holy Man's lurid personal habits and his wasteful and opulent lifestyle and left them at a junction not much further up. It was as simple as that. The Holy Man met his sad and ignominious end in the middle of a street somewhere, torn from limb to limb and his teeth smashed, completely unsuspecting. The Capitalist stood to one side and watched eagerly. The crowd kept pieces of his robe and some even took parts of his body for souvenirs. Oh, I suppose that in days gone by they might have erected a monument on the spot. But the expense would no longer justify the return on the investment. The notion of culture and history had only really been useful for attracting tourists, back in the day when there was a market for that kind of thing.

The Politician was neither surprised nor remorseful (perhaps a little, but nothing that he wasn't able to suppress with incidental ease) about the demise of his long-time partner, which just goes to show you how ignorant a man he really was. It seems that the Capitalist still had some small use for him, for it was the Politician who directed the construction of the Capitalist's new version of temples. For the Capitalist knew that until such time as he was able to wipe it from their nature, the workers had an innate need to satisfy their very human sense of spiritual longing. So, he designed massive standing formations made of the cheapest material possible and painted over with a shiny, golden paint that glittered even in the pollution-dampened sunlight and placed them in every worker's barracks. These were all identical and devoid of decoration and took the simple but easily recognizable form of the currency symbol of Oceania. The workers flocked to them to leave little notes or to pray that they would keep their jobs or, especially later, that the corporate farm in which they worked wouldn't be blown to bits anytime soon.

Now, about this time the Politician became aware of a very strange thing indeed. And that was this: no one came to see him anymore. No one asked him to sign documents and no one needed him to approve budgets or carry out any of the other administrative tasks he used to perform. To be sure, the building with the gates and the guards was a hive of activity. Directors scurried purposefully along the darkened hallways, seemingly on the verge of colliding into one another but somehow avoiding disaster. The Politician would stand among them, trying to catch one's attention on his way by and inquire as to what all the fuss was about, but no one bothered to look at him, never mind give a meaningful answer to his question. Perplexed, the Politician listened carefully to what they were saying. The directors would bark at each other even as they flitted by, and some could even be seen hurrying about in pairs. The directors all spoke in capital letters. Here are some of the things they said: "WE MUST INCREASE THE GENETIC SUPPLEMENT IN THE WORKERS' DIET", or "WE MUST REGULATE HOW MANY CHILDREN THE WORKERS HAVE UNTIL WE CAN ACTUALLY GROW THEM", or "OPINIONS AND BELIEFS OF ANY KIND ARE DANGEROUS". The Politician couldn't make much of it.

But after enough spying and snooping about the Politician eventually realized what was going on. The Capitalist, it seems, had taken it upon himself to contact his counterparts in Eurasia and Eastasia and pointing out the risks and expenses of constant, unmanaged warfare. Even if he appeared at the moment to be losing, the vicissitudes of Fortune, being what they were, by no means guaranteed their ultimate victory. Eventually, they agreed to a truce.

Imagine that! Without even the slightest involvement of the Politician, and here he was signing peace agreements! The Politician pouted and checked his head in the mirror. No, there it was. Perfect as always. Not a hair out of place. And that smile! Gorgeous as always. How could he have just circumvented him?

There was more bad news. It seems they had also agreed how useful the war had proven in managing their populations. The Politician remained ignorant of the details, but it seems they had agreed to resume hostilities some time in the future after the details had been worked out. The goal, however, was clear: perpetual warfare checked by stalemate.

Shaking his head, the Politician suspected there was something wrong with his information. It just didn't make sense. What was there to gain by it?

The Politician was crouched in his quarters, whispering hurriedly into his wrist, eyes roaming and jumping at the smallest noise outside, when someone caused the door to slide open. And what do you know? In strolled a compact robot, and trailing it a tall, rather nondescript young man who nodded his head enthusiastically at whatever the robot was saying. A look of sheer terror spread over the Politician's face. Abruptly, he cut the line and hoped for the best.

"Reaching out and trying to touch someone?" That voice, that sarcastic voice, was not his own, but the Politician knew exactly whose it was. He started to mumble some excuse, but the robot interrupted him. "No matter, and anyway I don't have time to listen to your pathetic excuses." The robot was a plain hunk of assorted types of plastic and was designed purely from a functional standpoint. Plain, angular, ugly even, it had large flat panels for eyes and strange flaps for ears, and it rolled about on a pedestal that contained a variety of programmable instruments. It was not, the Politician knew, the only one of its kind. All over Oceania a vast army of these robots stood idly by, waiting for the Capitalist to take over and – as he had proved himself so adept at doing – assuming control. "The director and myself" – the robot gestured awkwardly at the young man standing obsequiously behind him – "still have a great deal of ground to cover today. Isn't that so?"

"I HAVE A GREAT DEAL ON MY PLATE, YES, BUT IT'S ALWAYS A PLEASURE TO SERVE."

"As you can see these directors are more disposed to their functions than you or that overdressed peacock ever were. Wouldn't you say?"

The Politician was unable to answer. The awkward silence was eventually broken by the director.

"OF COURSE HE AGREES, SIR. YOU ARE, AFTER ALL, A GENIUS. I'M SURE THE GENTLEMEN IS MERELY OVERCOME BY YOUR TOWERING PRESENCE."

The robot hummed thoughtfully. "Yes, well, let's get down to business." A panel on his torso opened silently. Gently, a small tray emerged. On the tray was a neat arrangement of disturbing instruments of all shapes and sizes. But they all had this is common: on one end a comfortable, slip-proof grip and on the other some form of nasty, protrusive edge. Sharp, gleaming edges sometimes curving and squat wide ones with spikes. Some looked very handy for reaching behind obstacles like bones or vital organs and others – well, most of them didn't readily lend themselves to any appropriate use.

The director standing behind the robot smiled lustfully when he saw the instruments and took an inadvertent step closer. "The director here," began the robot, "is extremely adept at the use of these instruments. I could enumerate their various uses, but I'm sure you've heard it all before or seen it in the arena – ah, yes, of course, you've arranged a few of those spectacles yourself. There is, of course, no point in trying to impress you." At that the tray with the instruments receded into the robot's torso. All of them, that is, except for one rather simple instrument. It looked to be about the size and shape of a large but ordinary looking needle. "Anyway, the director will only be making use of this one." And at that, the robot picked up the instrument and handed it to the director, who received it gladly. "Be careful," joked the robot, "it's sharp!" The director giggled.

The robot turned its attention back to the Politician. The man was sagging to the floor. Desperate words were making their way slowly to his lips. They were having trouble cutting through the heavy blanket of dread and paralysis that choked him. He wanted to reason with him, he wanted to evoke memories of their charmed past together –

"No need to beg, really," the robot said. "It would be so demeaning. Anyway, I've already made up my mind. Loose ends do need tidying up.

"However, I have also decided to allow you to take matters into your own hands. Show a little initiative on your part. The director and I" – the robot made a small gesture - "have a small errand to take care of. Oh no, nothing that concerns you. But I imagine we'll be back in about fifteen minutes. If you are still alive at that time, I will be leaving the director and his handy instrument behind when I leave. Do I make myself understood?"

The Politician did not answer. He was unable.

The robot whirled about and headed for the door. "Fifteen minutes," it repeated, and then it was gone.

The director looked awkwardly at the Politician. "PLEASED TO MEET YOU," he offered, and when the Politician did not respond, he, too, left the room.

And so that was the end of the Politician. That was, in fact, the end of everything. We merely wait for the Universe to sweep up the mess and start all over again.

All those years we feared that we would blow ourselves to bits in some conflagration of our own making. Who ever would have suspected the truth? And so I ask you once again: did we arrive here by deliberate choice or did nature inadvertently introduce some subtle flaw in our genetic makeup that forced us here? Oh, I suppose the answer is irrelevant. I suppose it is both of them and none at all, in fact. Because the inevitability of the fact was proven when it came to pass. Choice is only choice at the moment of choosing.

We human beings share parts of the nature of a violent, territorial creature called the chimpanzee. But we also share parts of the nature of the bonobo, a social creature that was inclined towards contentment and derived pleasure from the company of its peers. Oh, even supposing that both natures are present in equal strength, in the end the forces of hatred – which we used to call "evil" – will always engulf those of love – which we used to call "good". For the forces of hatred are active, and the forces of love passive, and thus more easily swallowed up and devoured.

Still, even when the forces of hatred have overcome all resistance, the ever-present forces of love, drawing from some wellspring deep in the fabric of our being, eventually bubble up first here and then there and then, even as the forces of hatred rush about to squelch them, in a myriad of places all at once. At first tiny currents that gain in strength and join up with one another, and the battle of "good versus evil" is suddenly rejoined, and the cycle renewed.

A great deal of the lost folklore of humanity centered around this internal conflict. And as the technology at our command became more powerful, and because the persons who wielded power often arrived at their seats of might by injustice, we all thought the danger was that some man or woman, consumed by his own personal hatred, would press a button or let a few drops of liquid spill out of a vial, and bang! in a few miserable instants it would all be over.

We never reckoned on the Capitalist. A man who realized that it wasn't in his interests to allow us to blow ourselves up. No, he saw a better use for humanity. And he found a way to get us to go along with him. The fact never ceases to amaze me. The consumers were inclined to abandon the subtle and yet infinitely more satisfying rewards to be had from social contact in favor of the superficial and the more fleeting. Are we so

The Politics of Consumption

hierarchically and materialistically inclined that the choice was inevitable?

Millions of years ago, evolution experimented on this planet with large, powerful bodies and brute force. But those creatures, even if they did succeed in taking over the earth, were not able to perceive external threats such as, shall we say, the impact of a comet. So when evolution had to start all over again, she devised a new strategy. The sheer size and power of the bodies was reduced, and this time she gave us intelligence. Alas, she did not reckon with the possibility that the greatest danger threatening us lay inside our own heads. Or perhaps she did. Perhaps we were just an experiment. Perhaps we should take solace from the possibility that we were a step in her own learning curve – on the way to something greater.

And so now I must leave you. I can see by the look in your eye that I have disturbed you. I know that the first chance you'll get you'll turn me in. Go back, then, to your corporate farm and your barracks, remember to stay within the electronic perimeter of your sector unless you have permission. I must go. The electronic perimeter doesn't know me, not yet, it never has. When you return, you will feel better, and if they don't terminate you then tomorrow you will be back at your place in the factory, or sent on some suicide mission in Eurasia, and all the while you will be thinking what they have tacked up in huge, shiny letters above your barracks and in your workplace. Warm, welcome words are these, and I supposed it was foolish of me to try to supplant them. Yes, yes, my child, I can see them now, from here, even as we speak. Turn, look, yes, there. Ah, I can see you relax. It is the only truth you know.

WORK WILL SET YOU FREE.

Gyges the Terrible

Welcome to the United States of the not-so-distant future. Our Republic has given way to a new form of government, Freemocracy. The President rules virtually unopposed. Congress is a rubber-stamp institution, and society has fractured into the permanently privileged and the permanently working. The Supreme Court is the only alternate center of power, and the tension between the President, Samuel Judas Epstein, and the Chief Justice, Xiling, is set to boil over into open conflict.

The Earth, too, has changed. The nation has become a patchwork of restricted areas, security screens, and military checkpoints. Water is tightly rationed. The world powers vie with each other for territory on the lunar surface. Although the mines there are incredibly expensive to operate, the moon has become the only source for most of the natural resources consumed by an ever more ravenous industrial complex.

It is in this setting that a group of ordinary hooligans led by Marcellus Gyges storm the halls of empire. Possessed of a magic ring that confers the power of command, spurred on by his friends, Marcellus is in a unique position to depose the President.

At the same time, Marcellus is being tutored by his Guardian Angel. For it is the choices that we make in this life that determine what becomes of us in the next.

Thank You For Your Cooperation
the Bunker Series, #1

Welcome to the Bunker, an orderly, underground utopia where everyone's needs have been satisfied.

As far back as he can remember, Terry Renfield has been digging up uranium ore in the mines and getting into the occasional drunken brawl. Until one daystretch on the *Loyalty Stretch*, he and the rest of the Bunker see someone who looks eerily like himself commit a heinous act of treason. Terry is fired on the spot.

He turns to his girlfriend, Sally Xinhua, for help. Detained and then unexpectedly set free, Terry comes to realize that his misfortunes are no accident. His tiny, insular world shattered forever, he is determined not to be anyone's unwitting pawn – least of all his own.

Sally pulls him into the orbit of more privileged citizens with security clearances – including Van Johnson, the host of Ten Things I Hate About Treason, and Felix Tubman, the head of Homeland Security. What follows is an unlikely adventure spanning the Bunker, the reaches of space, and the forbidding outside.

Now the focus of a grand conspiracy to take down Control, the principal guiding force in the Bunker, Terry is ultimately faced with an identity crisis of epic proportions. Who is the *real* Terry Renfield? And what is it to actually *be* a specific person anyway?

ABOUT THE AUTHOR

Adam Wasserman took to writing at a young age and has never given it up. He has authored a number of short stories and plays but prefers the longer format and deeper potential of the novel.

Mr. Wasserman spends part of the year in Europe where he does most of his writing. During the spring and summer months, he can usually be found in Rhode Island. There, he attends numerous festivals and open markets – such as Providence ComiCon – where he enjoys engaging with readers. An avid swimmer, he also spends considerable time at the beach.

Topics that interest him include ancient history, power, and the nature of being human.

www.ingramcontent.com/pod-product-compliance
Lightning Source LLC
Chambersburg PA
CBHW022126170526
45157CB00004B/1777